"Works of art make rules; rules do not make works of art."

- Claude Debussy

Backstory

My name is Melvin Tellier, founder of Musiciangoods and author of Music Theory Simplified. My musical journey began in 2008 with a MIDI keyboard, headphones, and FL Studio. However, my first steps into the world of music trace back to my teenage years, when I took classical and electric guitar lessons. As my passion for music production grew, I began sharing my discoveries on YouTube under the alias "MellaMayne." If you were exploring music production between 2010 and 2015, you might have come across some of my tutorials.

Despite my love for music, I struggled with understanding music theory. As a self-taught musician, I pieced together knowledge from YouTube tutorials. While I managed to grasp the basics, more advanced concepts often seemed out of reach. After years of creating sample-based music, I began to feel constrained and decided to master music theory to expand my creative abilities. This journey culminated in my first book, Music Theory Simplified, focused on keyboard instruments.

The book was warmly received, and I'm grateful to have been able to help so many fellow musicians who share the same passion. Following its success, many readers requested a version specifically tailored for guitar. Having played guitar off and on for years, I'm well aware of the unique challenges guitarists face. Many guitarists, especially in younger generations, are self-taught, relying on shapes and positions rather than formal theory. Even legends like Jimi Hendrix, who wasn't formally trained, relied on a natural genius that most of us don't possess. While self-teaching can take you far, a solid understanding of theory can help unlock your full potential.

That's why I created Guitar Theory Simplified. This book is designed to be accessible and user-friendly, regardless of your skill level. It's packed with visuals, comparisons to piano, analogies, and cheat sheets—all aimed at making guitar theory easier to understand, so you can fully realize your musical potential. I also recommend checking out our Guitar Theory Cheat Sheet, available on our website, which complements the book perfectly.

Whether you're just starting out or have been playing for years, I invite you to join me on this journey. Together, we'll break down the complexities of guitar theory and turn it into a tool that enhances your playing. Let's make guitar theory simple—because understanding what you're playing shouldn't be a mystery. I'm excited to see where this journey will take you!

How this book will help you

The debate over the necessity of music theory in crafting exceptional music is a topic of ongoing discussion in the music world. Drawing from my own experiences as a music producer, I can confirm the significant advantages that a solid understanding of music theory can bring to one's creative work. While not an absolute requirement for music production, I believe it plays a crucial role in enhancing creative output.

I remember a time when I produced music without formal music theory knowledge, resulting in somewhat rudimentary compositions and a feeling of creative limitation.

Having an understanding of music theory is akin to musical literacy. Without it, interpreting music is like trying to read a book solely through its pictures – you may get a sense of the story, but you'll miss the intricacies. If you aim to become a proficient musician, gaining a foundation in music theory is essential for achieving musical literacy.

Once you attain this musical literacy, everything falls into place. You gain a deeper understanding of your compositions and other songs, facilitating communication and collaboration with fellow musicians. You'll break free from reliance on samples or limited chord progressions, ultimately removing barriers to your musical growth.

In this book, we approach music theory differently, using clear illustrations and analogies to ensure a comprehensive understanding of these concepts. Our goal is to equip you with a thorough understanding so you can readily apply it to your music, whether you're pursuing a music career or exploring music as a hobby.

This isn't your typical music theory book. As I mentioned earlier, we've stripped away all the extraneous concepts, zeroing in on the ideas that will truly empower you to turn your creative visions into music.

Our book is meticulously crafted for ease of understanding. We present information visually, sparing you the need to sift through pages laden with text. It's a straightforward, essential guide that gets right to the heart of the matter.

How the book is structured

In creating this book, our goal was to adopt a fresh and effective approach to learning guitar theory. We've carefully selected nine fundamental concepts that we believe are essential for building the knowledge needed to create music from scratch on the guitar.

While you may already know this, it's worth emphasizing: music theory and guitar theory are essentially the same. The difference lies in how music theory is applied to the guitar. Due to its unique layout, the application differs from that of a keyboard instrument. Traditional music theory is often explained using a piano or keyboard because its layout makes complex concepts easier to visualize and understand. For this reason, we've chosen to use the piano keyboard as a reference point while explaining these theory concepts in the context of the guitar.

As you move through the book, you'll find that the concepts gradually delve deeper into music theory. For example, in the first chapter, we introduce the musical alphabet, explore note names, and explain half steps and whole steps. By the final chapter, we'll have demystified the circle of fifths. This structured approach ensures that you start with the basics and progressively build your knowledge. Each of the nine theory concepts is dedicated to its own chapter, with bite-sized lessons that break down every aspect of the concept in detail.

To make learning easier, we've included plenty of visuals. Each concept is accompanied by a graph or diagram, which also doubles as a handy cheat sheet that you can refer to anytime. At the beginning of each chapter, you'll find an estimated completion time and a list of tools you'll need to fully engage with the material.

To further enrich your learning experience, we've incorporated QR codes throughout the book. Scanning these codes will take you to our website, where you'll find video tutorials featuring me breaking down each concept in a comprehensive and engaging way.

QR Codes included

Scan the QR code to access our video tutorial for the corresponding lesson.

How to read our graphs

In this book, we frequently use piano and guitar illustrations, along with graphs, to help you grasp theory concepts on both instruments. In the early chapters, notes will be shown on each instrument by their note names. As you become more comfortable with these names, we'll introduce finger positions for each note, guiding you on which fingers to use on specific frets and strings.

Fretboard illustrations and symbols

This book uses both horizontal and vertical fretboard illustrations to clarify guitar concepts. An "X" indicates a string that should not be played, while an "O" marks an open string to be played without fretting. Position markers are shown as circles and numbers on the 3rd, 5th, 7th, 9th, and 12th frets, with the 12th fret typically marked by two circles.

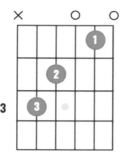

Finger positions

When there are no finger numbers provided, align each finger with a fret, ensuring minimal movement across the fretboard. Use the closest finger to the note's fret position, follow standard scale or chord patterns, and prioritize comfort for smooth playing. Regular practice will help you instinctively choose the best finger placements.

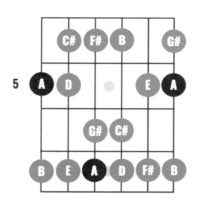

Finger numbering

To ensure you use the correct fingers on the corresponding frets and strings, we use numbers to indicate finger placement. "1" represents the index finger, "2" the middle finger, "3" the ring finger, and "4" the pinky finger.

Final thoughts

Before we delve into the lessons, I'd like to share some final thoughts. It's essential to recognize that music, at its core, consists of nothing more than notes—whether they are played individually or simultaneously. Music, in its essence, is simply a collection of notes. It's crucial not to over-complicate it.

If you ever find yourself struggling to grasp a musical concept, try to simplify it in your mind as nothing more than notes. This approach has helped me maintain a sense of simplicity in music, even when faced with intimidating compositions or moments of confusion.

Ultimately, your success in mastering these concepts depends on your determination to learn. We have strived to make this book as straightforward and digestible as possible, but you still need to invest the time to read and engage with the content to fully understand it.

Take your time as you work through this book. Proceed through each chapter at your own pace. If you ever encounter doubts about a particular concept, don't hesitate to revisit that chapter. Unless you already have a solid grasp of a concept, ensure you thoroughly understand it before moving on to the next chapter.

The structure of this book is linear, meaning you should advance to the next chapter only when you feel prepared. Our goal is for you to comprehend every aspect thoroughly, as even seemingly less important subjects play a vital role.

Avoid skipping chapters based on assumptions of prior knowledge, as this might lead to confusion in subsequent chapters. So, let go of any ego, find a comfortable space, eliminate distractions, and prepare to immerse yourself fully in each lesson.

Upon completing this book, you will have earned the right to call yourself a *literate musician*, whether you pursue playing guitar or piano as a hobby, DJ on weekends, or aspire to sell your beats as a music producer. Your journey towards musical proficiency begins here.

Table of contents

1. THE PIANO
FUNDAMENTALS

Before we dive into guitar theory, it's beneficial to start with the fundamentals of the piano. Understanding the piano provides a solid foundation for grasping music theory concepts.

In this chapter, we will explore the essential elements of the piano. You will gain a comprehensive understanding of the keyboard's layout and learn to recognize recurring patterns.

Additionally, you will become familiar with the names of each note and the intervals between them. After this initial introduction, we will explain how these concepts apply to the guitar.

‹ WHAT YOU WILL LEARN

- The 12 note pattern
- The Note names
- Half/whole steps

‹ WHAT DO YOU NEED

- Piano or MIDI Keyboard
- Whiteboard markers
- A smartphone

‹ SKIP THIS LESSON IF

- You already play piano
- You know the note names
- You know the intervals

Introduction to the piano

If you're an absolute beginner with no experience playing the keyboard or guitar, we'll start from the very basics. We'll begin with the piano, as it provides the clearest foundation for understanding music theory. After this introductory chapter, we will delve into guitar theory. If you're already familiar with the piano keyboard, you can skip this chapter.

You might wonder why a guitar theory book includes information about the piano. The reason is that traditional music theory is much easier to understand on the piano keyboard. The piano's linear layout, with notes arranged sequentially and repeating in clear patterns, simplifies the explanation of musical concepts compared to the guitar. Therefore we frequently use piano images throughout this book, to simplify certain concepts. Or as a reference.

This chapter is designed for those who have never played the piano or are unfamiliar with its layout. By the end of this chapter, you will have a solid understanding of the piano keyboard, which is crucial for comprehending guitar theory.

We strongly recommend starting with the piano keyboard for anyone new to music, regardless of the instrument you plan to play. It's not necessary to become proficient in playing the piano, but understanding its layout and how it works is essential when learning music theory.

Throughout this book, you will see top-down images of a piano keyboard or a guitar fretboard with notes highlighted. The green highlights or circles show the keys played in the image, we start most examples on the key of C4 , where the middle C is. Since a full-range keyboard has 88 keys, this is key 40.

Highlighted keyboard

The 12-note pattern

Let's take a closer look at the piano keyboard. Pianos come in various sizes, each with a different number of keys. Small MIDI controllers might have 25 keys, while others come with 49 or 61 keys. A full-sized piano keyboard, however, boasts 88 keys. The greater the number of keys, the wider the range of pitches available. At first glance, the keyboard might seem simple—a series of white and black keys, right?

But when you examine it more closely, you'll realize there's a bit more to it. Keeping track of all the keys and deciphering the patterns between the white and black keys can be confusing. So, let's break it down.

First and foremost, it's important to know that although a full piano keyboard has 88 keys, there are only 12 unique notes. These 12 notes are the foundation of every musical composition, across all instruments.

Understanding this concept is crucial. No matter the genre—whether it's hip-hop, jazz, pop, classical, or anything in between—all the sounds you hear in any song come from these same 12 notes. Think of it like a painter's palette. Just as a painter works with a limited set of colors to create a masterpiece, musicians use these 12 notes to craft every piece of music. The pattern begins at C and continues up the keyboard, including the black keys, until it repeats at the next C. This pattern is also called the chromatic scale. We'll dive deeper into this pattern soon.

12-note pattern

The pattern repeats

Now, let's consider the inclusion of a piano with 88 keys. How does it fit into the overall picture? The great news is that the same 12-note pattern we discussed earlier remains applicable to an 88-key keyboard. This pattern effortlessly repeats itself across the entire span of the keyboard.

Getting to know the 12-note pattern helps you navigate the piano and its notes more easily. The pattern repeats at different octaves, changing the note's pitch. Moving lower makes the notes lower in pitch, and going higher makes them higher. The same way as notes get higher when you move higher up your guitar's fretboard.

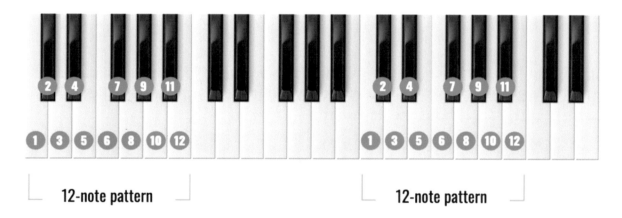

12-note pattern   12-note pattern

An 88-key MIDI keyboard is versatile. You can play deep bass tones on the lower octaves and melodic elements on the higher ones. The same C note sounds the same, whether in the middle or two octaves down, with only a pitch difference.

Octave C1-C2   Octave C3-C4

Identifying patterns

Recognizing the 12-note patterns becomes much simpler when you employ a color-coded layout on the piano keyboard. However, attempting to paint the piano yourself is not recommended (though piano stickers can be a helpful alternative if needed).

Fortunately, there are simpler methods to identify your position on the piano by observing the arrangement of black and white keys. The piano has a distinctive pattern of white keys that was specifically designed to facilitate navigation.

When you're just starting out, it's completely normal to feel a bit confused when looking at a piano keyboard. In due time, however, you'll be able to make sense of it all. For now, it's beneficial to focus on the black keys.

Take a look at the piano, and you'll notice groups of black keys arranged in a repeated pattern across the keyboard. These groups consist of two black keys followed by three black keys. This pattern continues consistently throughout the keyboard.

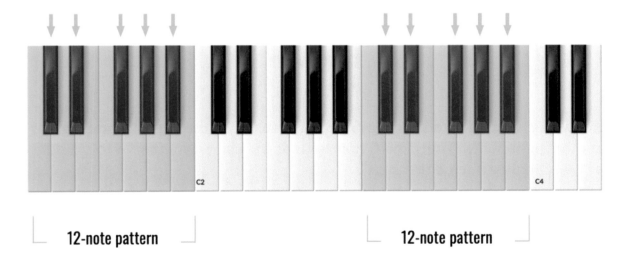

12-note pattern   12-note pattern

By familiarizing yourself with this *2-3 pattern*, you can gain a deeper understanding of the keyboard layout and the relationships between notes. The consistent arrangement of black keys serves as a valuable reference point for identifying and playing different musical intervals, scales, and chords.

Black keys are markers

The black keys on the piano mark important 12-note patterns. Their color, size, position, and tactile feel distinguish them from white keys, helping you navigate the keyboard. Without these distinctions, finding your place on the piano would be challenging!

To start, find any pair of black keys. They are surrounded by three white keys. The leftmost white key in this group is the first note of the 12-note pattern.

Now, look at the group of three black keys to the right. There are four white keys around this cluster. The rightmost white key in this setup marks the last key of the 12-note pattern.

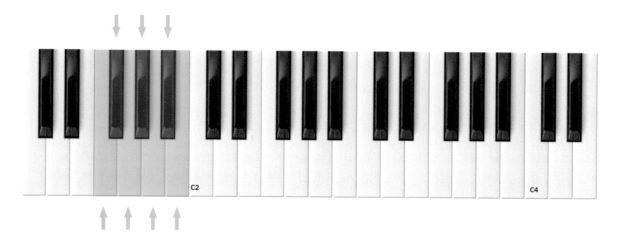

See for yourself

When we combine all the information, this is what we find. Across the entire span of an 88-key piano, you can observe the complete set of 12-note patterns. These patterns consist of either two black keys with three surrounding white notes, and three black keys with four surrounding white notes.

12-note pattern

By understanding this repetitive pattern, you gain the ability to navigate the piano with ease. Here's an example of the pattern across a four-octave keyboard:

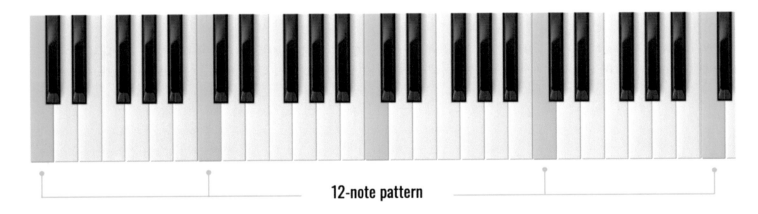

12-note pattern

By now, you should have a basic understanding of piano keys, their symbols, and structure. In the next chapter, we'll dive deeper into note names. But before moving on, let's recap what we've just covered.

In short

Kudos on your grasp of the significant 12-note pattern on the piano keyboard! Through your ability to recognize the visual patterns created by the black keys, you can effortlessly identify these patterns across the entire keyboard. It is crucial to acknowledge that the entirety of music is constructed using only these 12 distinct keys.

These keys generate striking visual patterns that consistently repeat themselves throughout the piano. Each 12-note pattern consists of a set of two black keys, a set of three black keys, and the white notes encompassing them. Having understood this concept, it is now time to embark on the next phase and acquaint ourselves with the designated names assigned to each individual note. Let's delve right in!

The 12 key pattern

The identification of the 12-note pattern on your piano keyboard relies on recognizing the visual patterns formed by the black keys. Remember all of music comes from just twelve notes.

Unique keys

Every one of the twelve notes or keys on the piano produces its distinct sound, making each of them unique.

Visual patterns

The 12 keys create distinct visual patterns that repeat themselves across the keyboard.

Groups of keys

Each 12-note pattern on the piano consists of a group of two black keys, a group of three black keys, and the surrounding white notes.

Exercise the pattern

While it's not necessary to learn to play the piano to understand guitar theory, practicing the 12-note pattern on a piano can be very helpful. Here's a simple exercise to help you get started. This exercise will train your eyes and fingers to recognize and navigate the 12-note pattern on the piano keyboard. Regular practice will enhance your overall familiarity with the keyboard and improve your ability to play melodies, chords, and progressions with ease.

● Start by familiarizing yourself with the groups of black keys and their corresponding white keys. Remember that there are two black keys followed by three black keys, and this pattern repeats across the keyboard.

● Begin playing the pattern from any starting point. For example, locate a group of two black keys and identify the leftmost white key. This will be your starting note and it will always be a C note.

● Play the sequence of 12 notes by moving to the right, following the pattern of black and white keys. Play each key until you reach the rightmost white key of the pattern.

● Repeat this exercise in both directions, moving from left to right and right to left across the keyboard.

● As you become more comfortable with the exercise, try playing the pattern starting from different positions on the keyboard. This will help reinforce your understanding of the 12-note pattern and its repetition.

● Remember to take your time and play at a pace that allows you to accurately identify and play each note. Gradually increase your speed as you become more proficient.

The note names

Now that we have identified the 12 keys or notes used in creating music, let's assign names to these notes to make them easier to remember. To begin, we will focus on the white keys, which will serve as a foundation for learning the black notes.

Naming the piano notes is (almost) as simple as reciting the alphabet. You are likely familiar with the letters A to G, and we will utilize these letters to assign names to the piano notes. This straightforward approach is possible due to the repeating patterns we discussed in the previous chapter. The pattern of notes on the piano keyboard repeats itself, and so do the note names. The sequence of note names is as follows: **A-B-C-D-E-F-G**, collectively known as the "natural" keys.

The key of C
Notice that the first note of the piano is C, while the last one before reaching the next C is B. This is why many instructional books and tutorials often use the key of C when teaching. Each note following C has a progressively higher pitch, while each note below C has a lower pitch.

ABCDEFG
The pattern repeats across the entire piano keyboard, spanning multiple octaves. As you descend, the notes sound lower, and as you ascend, the pitches become higher but we use the same letter to identify notes across different parts of the keyboard.

← Lower pitches   Higher pitches →

17

The black keys

Now let's explore the names of the black keys on the piano keyboard. In essence, the names of the black keys are closely related to the names of the white keys. However, there is a catch. The black keys can be viewed as modifications or variations of the adjacent white notes, representing higher or lower pitched versions of those notes.

In music, we take small steps left or right on the piano. Moving right from a white key to a black key sharpens the note (e.g., C to C#), raising its pitch. Moving left from a white key to a black key flattens the note (e.g., D to Db), lowering its pitch. The black key between C and D can be called C# or Db, which are called 'enharmonic equivalents' representing the same note.

Naming black keys

The black keys can be called either C# D#, F#, G# and A# when the black key is located higher than the white key or they can be named: Db, Eb, Gb, Ab and Bb when they are lower than their closest white key. In the diagram on the right you can see how this works.

← Lower black keys are called flats (b)

→ Higher black keys are called sharps (#)

Enharmonic equivalent

Not only black keys can be changed with sharps (#) or flats (b) in their names; this can also affect white keys. For instance, when you add a sharp (#) to E, it becomes the note that's usually called F. Therefore, F and E# are enharmonic equivalents. In music, a sharp or flat is really just a notation used to raise or lower a note's pitch.

Enharmonic equivalent

In short

Great! You have now familiarized yourself with the names of the notes on the piano keyboard, which follow a simple alphabetical pattern: A-B-C-D-E-F-G. These notes repeat themselves across the keyboard, creating a consistent and predictable pattern.

By understanding these fundamental concepts of note names and their relationships, you are well-equipped to delve further into the captivating world of music theory. So, keep these key concepts in mind as we continue into piano intervals.

A-B-C-D-E-F-G

The musical notes on the piano are represented by the letters A, B, C, D, E, F, and G. This sequence of notes begins with C and ends with B, after which it repeats again, maintaining the same alphabetical order. This recurring pattern allows you to easily navigate the keyboard and identify notes.

Modifications

Black keys on the piano are modifications of the adjacent white notes. They serve as intermediate steps between the white keys and can be referred to as sharp (#) or flat (b) notes. A black key can have two names depending on its context and relationship to the neighboring white keys. When you go up, their called sharps. When you go down, their called flats.

Enharmonic equivalent

Enharmonic equivalents are two different notations (or spellings) for the same musical pitch. They represent the same sound on an instrument but may be written differently in sheet music. For example, C# and Db are enharmonic equivalents because they produce the same piano key or note, even though they are written differently.

Exercise the note names

Here are some simple exercises to help you memorize piano note names. Remember to practice these exercises regularly and be patient with yourself.

It takes time and repetition to become comfortable with piano note names. With consistent practice, you'll gradually improve your ability to identify and recall the names of the notes on the piano keyboard.

- Play and say: Play random white keys and say their names out loud.

- Note matching: Match written note names to the corresponding keys on the piano.

- Note recognition: Practice naming notes as you play them in specific areas of the keyboard.

- Note speed drill: Name as many notes as possible within a set time limit.

- Note patterns: Identify and name notes within common patterns on the piano.

Whole steps

In our previous lesson, we explored the piano with 12-note patterns and how to recognize them on your piano keyboard. We introduced the letter names assigned to both the white and black keys, noticing the distinctive grouping of the black keys into sets of two or three. Now, it's time to head into the concept of half steps and whole steps.

Half steps and whole steps are crucial elements in understanding the musical intervals between notes. A half step, also known as a *semitone*, refers to the smallest possible distance between two adjacent keys on the piano keyboard, (or frets on the guitar fretboard), whether they are white or black keys. This interval encompasses the distance between any two consecutive keys, such as from C to C#, D to D#, and so on.

Whole steps

On the other hand, a whole step, also referred to as a **whole tone**, represents a larger interval comprising two consecutive half steps, or two frets on the guitar fretboard. In simpler terms, it encompasses the distance of two keys, whether they are adjacent white keys or include a black key in between, such as from C to D, D to E, and so forth.

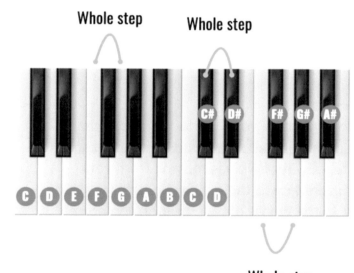

To move a whole step, you skip one key to reach the next. Pairs of white keys separated by a black key (A-B, C-D, D-E, F-G, G-A) are all a whole step apart. Practice by counting two keys to the right. A whole step above E is the black key next to F, and a whole step above B is the black key next to C.

21

Half steps

A half step, or semitone, is the smallest musical interval between two notes. On a piano keyboard, it's the distance between adjacent keys and on the guitar, between adjacent frets. Most white keys have a black key to their right (a half step above) and a black key to their left (a half step below).

For example, if you take the note G on the piano keyboard, the black key to its upper right is positioned "in between" the notes G and A. This black key is considered a half step above G and a half step below A.

However, there are two pairs of white keys, namely E/F and B/C, that do not have black keys in between them. This is because the intervals between E and F, as well as between B and C, are already half steps in themselves.

Half steps

To your right, you'll find a piano diagram illustrating half steps. Notice that a half step always involves moving from your current key to the one immediately beside it. In the words of MJ, "It doesn't matter if it's black or white."

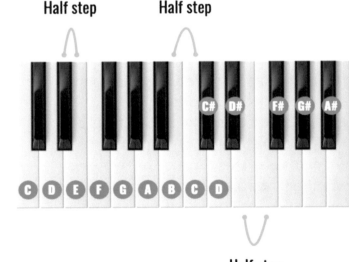

While it may appear elementary or repetitive, grasping the concept of whole steps and half steps is crucial for constructing scales, chords, and chord progressions. The same applies for guitar. More on that later.

Key takeaways

When playing the piano or guitar, the journey from one note to another involves taking small steps known as half steps and whole steps. These steps, both in terms of their physical distance on the keyboard/fretboard and their musical interval, are fundamental to understanding the concept of scales and constructing them on the piano or guitar.

To familiarize yourself with these steps, it is beneficial to practice on your own piano keyboard. As you play, observe the arrangement of keys and notice the different intervals between them. You will discover that some steps feel closer together, while others require stretching or moving your hand to reach the next note.

Half step

On the piano, a half step above a key is the key to its immediate right, while a half step below a key is the key to its immediate left. On the guitar, it is the immediate left or right fret.

Whole step

A whole step on the piano is two keys to the right, or two keys to the left. On the guitar, it is two frets to the left or right.

Enharmonic equivalent

As you explore the piano keyboard, and later the guitar fretboard, you may observe that each key or fret can have multiple names, and this is because certain notes possess enharmonic equivalence, which means they are spelled differently but produce the same sound. An example of this is the notes C sharp and D flat, which are enharmonically equivalent.

Jargon guide

Music theory can be a complex subject, and even more so with its specialized vocabulary. This guide is here to assist you in comprehending and defining the terms you've come across in this chapter or to refresh your memory.

The 12-key pattern

The 12 key pattern refers to the arrangement of musical keys within the Western tonal system, consisting of the major and minor keys that span all 12 pitch classes in an octave.

DAW

A digital audio workstation (DAW) is a software application used for recording, editing, and producing digital audio files, typically offering a wide range of tools and features for music production and sound design.

Note

A note is a symbolic representation of a specific pitch and duration in music, typically written on a staff and indicating the fundamental building block of melody and harmony.

Middle

Middle C is the musical pitch located near the center of a piano keyboard and it is the 40th key. C is often used as a reference point in music notation.

Sharps and flats

Sharps and flats are symbols used in music notation to raise or lower the pitch of a note by a semitone, respectively, providing flexibility in expressing different tonalities and key signatures.

Musical alphabet

The musical alphabet refers to the sequence of letter names used to label the different pitches in Western music, spanning from A to G and repeating cyclically.

Pitch

A pitch on the piano refers to the specific frequency or perceived musical tone produced by striking a key on the instrument. The higher up you go, the higher the pitch will be. Vice versa for the lower you go.

Intervals

Intervals on the piano refer to the distance or relationship between two pitches, measured in terms of the number of keys or semitones between them, and are essential for understanding harmony, melody, and chord progressions.

2. THE GUITAR FUNDAMENTALS

Now that you've familiarized yourself with the piano keyboard, its 12-note pattern, note names, intervals, and sharps and flats, it's time to apply this knowledge to the guitar.

Everything we just covered also applies to the guitar, as well as any other instrument. The only difference is how the notes are played and their layout. Due to the guitar's unique layout, finding the notes differs from the piano.

In this chapter, we will show you the musical alphabet on a guitar fretboard, the note names, half steps, and whole steps. We'll also teach you how to identify the notes across your guitar's fretboard.

‹ WHAT YOU WILL LEARN

- The musical alphabet
- The Note names
- Half/whole steps
- The guitar fretboard

‹ WHAT DO YOU NEED

- Any 6 string guitar
- Whiteboard markers
- A smartphone

‹ SKIP THIS LESSON IF

- You know the musical alphabet
- You know the note names
- You know what intervals are
- You know the guitar fretboard

The guitar strings

Let's start with the basics: the guitar strings. When you pluck a string, it produces a note with a specific pitch and duration. Pressing down on a fret raises the pitch of the note. By pressing multiple frets and plucking their strings, you can form chords, playing multiple notes simultaneously.

Guitar strings are numbered from the thickest and lowest (6) to the thinnest and highest (1). In standard tuning, they are **E** (6), **A** (5), **D** (4), **G** (3), **B** (2), and **E** (1). There are two octaves between the open 6th string (E) and the open 1st string (E), meaning the musical alphabet cycle repeats twice.

Open strings produce specific notes and pressing the frets changes the pitch. Each string is positioned over frets, which function like piano keys. Playing the 6th string at the first and second frets moves up in half steps. As you move to thinner strings, the pitch gets higher.

Think of guitar strings as piano keyboards, each starting at a different note. To remember the order, use the mnemonic: **"Eddie Ate Dynamite, Good Bye Eddie."**

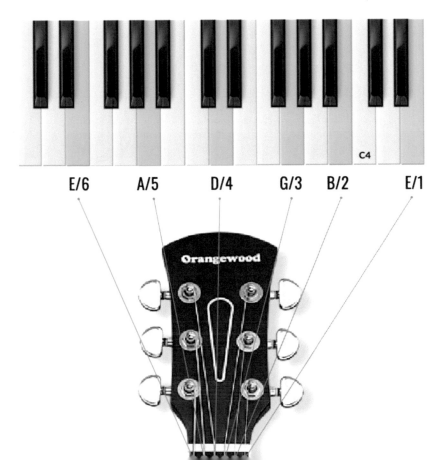

Piano vs guitar

To better understand the layout of the guitar fretboard, let's compare it to the layout of a piano keyboard to highlight the differences. By examining both, we can see how the linear arrangement of notes on the piano contrasts with the segmented and repetitive structure of the guitar fretboard. This comparison will help clarify how each instrument maps out the musical alphabet and how notes are organized and played.

Now, let's take another look at the piano keyboard to see how many keys you need to play to get from one A to the next A. This span includes eight white keys, but we must also consider the black keys in between. Including the black keys, there are 12 half steps in total. On a guitar fretboard, although there are no physical black keys, if we needed to move a certain amount of keys on the piano up or down to reach a note, the same amount of frets are needed on the guitar to reach the same note.

One octave on piano

The image illustrates the seamless transition from one A to the next, all you have to do is find the next white key in between the last two black keys. However, doing the same isn't as straightforward on a guitar. To highlight the complexity guitarists encounter when traversing the musical alphabet along a single string, we'll focus on the 5th string (A), which is tuned to the note A.

Octave A1-A2

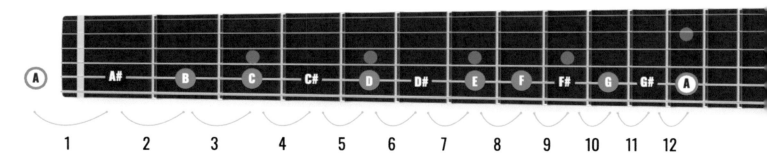

An octave spans eight musical alphabet letters, counting only white keys, which simplifies note memorization. On the guitar fretboard, an octave spans 12 frets on a single string, but its layout is less visually obvious compared to a keyboard. It's important to account for the equivalent of "black

Skipping frets

In the previous lesson, we learned the notes the guitar strings can produce, named according to the musical alphabet. To better understand their relationships, we need to grasp intervals, measured in whole steps and half steps. We'll explore these concepts further by examining their representation on the guitar fretboard.

The guitar fretboard combines the white and black keys of the piano into a continuous row on each string, similar to six overlapping piano keyboards, making it challenging to memorize.

Looking at the image from our last lesson, you'll see that notes on the guitar fretboard are not evenly spaced, except for B to C and E to F, which lack black keys on the piano and therefore have no gap on the fretboard.

To play the musical alphabet (A-B-C-D-E-F-G) on the guitar, you must skip the black keys. It's crucial to know where gaps occur in the musical alphabet and where they don't. Regardless of your position on the guitar fretboard, there will always be a fret's gap between the notes of the musical alphabet, except between B and C, and E and F, since these notes are just a semitone apart.

Musical alphabet on piano
On the right, you can see the musical alphabet on a piano keyboard. By playing only the white keys and avoiding the black keys, you can easily move from one A to the next A. This simplicity makes it easy to locate notes on a piano keyboard.

Musical alphabet

Skipping frets
However, on a guitar, the sequence is different. Without black keys, you need to skip a fret for each black key you would encounter on a piano keyboard.

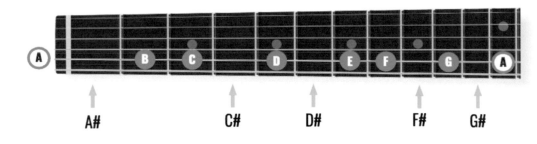

Whole steps

So in summary, for each note that is followed by a flat or sharp (i.e., a black key on the piano), you must skip a fret on the guitar. The only exceptions are B and E, as these notes are not followed by a black key on the piano keyboard. With this understanding, we can now introduce the concept of intervals.

In music, as we've shown you on piano in the previous chapter, we move in small steps up and down the fretboard or piano keyboard, and these steps are called intervals. The distance of two frets on the same string (e.g., A to B or C to D) is known as a whole step or whole tone.

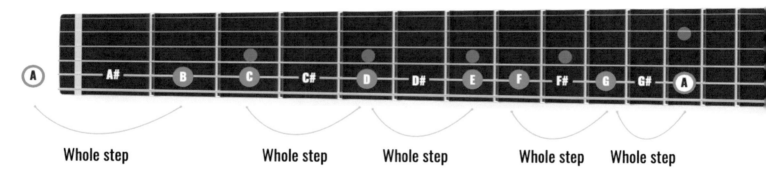

Whole step from an open string
A whole step above an open string is located at the 2nd fret. For instance, starting from the open 3rd string (G), the note A is found at the 2nd fret.

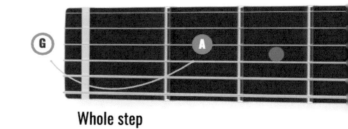

Whole step between strings
You can move a whole step vertically between strings, but this depends on the tuning intervals. For example, from the A note on the 5th fret of the 6th string (E), you can find the B note either by moving up a whole step to the 7th fret of the same string or by moving down to the 2nd fret of the 5th string (A).

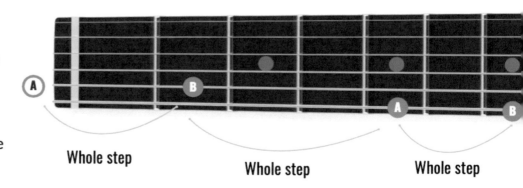

Half steps

Now that we covered the concept of whole steps (or whole tones), we're gonna introduce you to half-steps. Understanding both whole and half-step intervals is essential for building scales and transitioning between chords on the guitar.

A distance of one fret is called a half step or semitone. Consequently, a half step above an open string is located at the 1st fret. For instance, a half step above the open 2nd string (B) is the note C at the 1st fret.

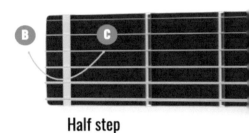

Half step

You can move a half step up (towards the guitar body) or down (towards the headstock) from any fret on the same string. Moving a half step between strings requires knowing the tuning intervals; which we'll teach you later. Typically, this involves moving to an adjacent string and adjusting frets accordingly.

For example, from the B note on the 7th fret of the 6th string (E), you can find the C note by moving up to the 8th fret. Alternatively, you can find the C note by moving down to the 3rd fret of the 5th string (A). However, remember this method doesn't always work seamlessly due to differences in string tuning.

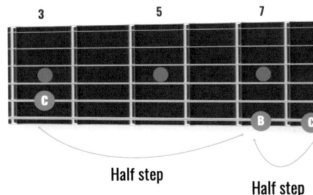

Half step

Half step

Half steps are straightforward to execute on a guitar compared to a piano. This is because a guitar doesn't have black keys. Moving up or down one fret on the guitar equals a half step. Skipping a fret results in a whole step.

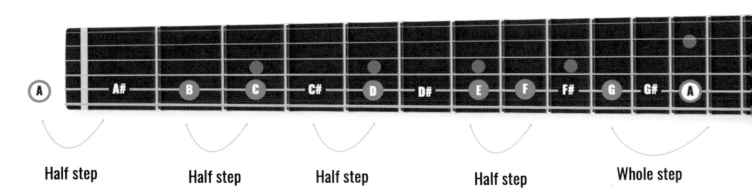

Half step   Half step   Half step   Half step   Whole step

Understanding the fretboard

Now that you understand half steps and whole steps on the guitar, it's time to identify the notes on the fretboard. This will give you a clearer picture of each note's location and make the overall concept more comprehensible.

It's important to memorize the guitar fretboard thoroughly, which means knowing every note on every fret and string. While this might seem daunting, it's actually manageable with practice. As a beginner, you can use markers or stickers to help you memorize the notes more easily.

One effective way to learn the notes on your fretboard is by using the chromatic scale. In traditional Western music theory, the chromatic scale includes all 12 notes available. Starting with a C note, the scale is as follows: C, C#/Db, D, D#/Eb, E, F, F#/Gb, G, G#/Ab, A, A#/Bb, B, and then back to C. This pattern repeats itself regardless of the starting note, with each note being one fret apart.

So, how does this help us learn the fretboard? Pick any note. For example, if you play the note on the fifth fret of the A string, according to the chart, that's a D. What would the note on the eighth fret be? Knowing the chromatic scale, you'll see that three notes up from D is F. Once you memorize the chromatic scale, identifying the notes on the guitar fretboard will become much easier.

Fretboard notes

As you can see, the black notes on this diagram represent the sharps/flats. These notes can be either a sharp or a flat, depending on whether you are moving up or down the fretboard. For example, moving up the fretboard from a natural note makes the next note a sharp, while moving down makes it a flat. After the 12th fret, the notes repeat themselves.

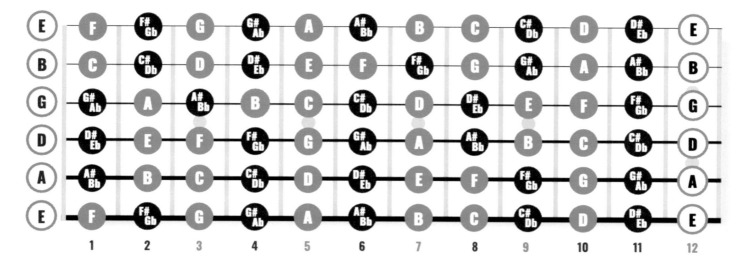

Exercises to learn the fretboard

While learning the notes on the guitar fretboard may seem challenging, a systematic approach makes it much more manageable. It's crucial to learn the notes because everything you do on the guitar, from playing scales to building chords, is based on knowing the fretboard. Without this knowledge, you'll limit your potential. Here are some effective methods to help you learn the notes on the fretboard quickly:

- **Learn the Open Strings:** Start by memorizing the notes of the open strings: E, A, D, G, B, E

- **Learn the Natural Notes on the Low E and A Strings:** Familiarize yourself with the natural notes (A, B, C, D, E, F, G) on the low E (6th) and A (5th) strings up to the 12th fret.

- **Use the Chromatic Scale:** Understand the chromatic scale, which includes all 12 notes: C, C#/Db, D, D#/Eb, E, F, F#/Gb, G, G#/Ab, A, A#/Bb, B. Each fret represents a half step, or one note in the chromatic scale.

- **Memorize Key Frets:** Memorize the notes on key frets such as the 3rd, 5th, 7th, 9th, and 12th frets.

- **Practice Octave Shapes:** Learn the shapes that help you find octaves on the fretboard.

- **Use Mnemonic Devices:** Create mnemonics or phrases to remember the order of notes.

- **Apply the Notes:** Play scales, chords, and arpeggios while saying the note names out loud.

- **Use Visual Aids:** Consider using fretboard diagrams or apps that provide visual references for note locations.

- **Practice Regularly:** Consistent practice is key. Spend a few minutes each day quizzing yourself on different fret positions and their corresponding notes.

Key takeaways

In this lesson, we explored the fundamental concepts of guitar music theory. We introduced you to the notes of your guitar strings, familiarized you with the musical alphabet from which all music derives, and explained the concepts of flats and sharps. We also compared the layout of the guitar fretboard to that of a piano, and taught you how music works in half and whole steps, helping you find the notes on your fretboard. Let's summarize the key takeaways:

The musical alphabet

The musical alphabet is the foundation of all music. It is a sequence of notes that repeats itself across a piano keyboard or a guitar fretboard. The sequence begins at A and continues through G, then repeats at a higher pitch each time an octave is reached. The sequence is: **A-B-C-D-E-F-G**

Flats and sharps

To understand music, it's helpful to start by looking at a piano keyboard. The black keys between the white keys represent what we call flats and sharps. These flats and sharps adjust the pitch of the adjacent white keys, making them either higher or lower. Although a guitar fretboard doesn't have physical black keys, we still need to consider these notes when playing guitar, as they are an essential part of music.

Half and whole steps

In music, we measure the distance between notes in steps, specifically half steps (semitones) and whole steps (whole tones). These steps are crucial for forming chords and scales. Whether you're learning guitar or any other instrument, understanding half and whole steps is a foundational aspect of music theory.

The fretboard

Your fretboard is your palette for writing and creating music. Each fret functions like a key on a piano. Moving from one fret to the next raises the pitch by a half step, while skipping a fret raises it by a whole step.

Jargon guide

Music theory can be a complex subject, and even more so with its specialized vocabulary. This guide is here to assist you in comprehending and defining the terms you've come across in this chapter or to refresh your memory.

Note

A note is a symbolic representation of a specific pitch and duration in music, typically written on a staff and indicating the fundamental building block of melody and harmony.

Pitch

A pitch on the piano refers to the specific frequency or perceived musical tone produced by striking a key on the instrument. The higher up you go, the higher the pitch will be. Vice versa for the lower you go.

Fret

A fret is a raised metal strip on the guitar neck that runs perpendicular to the strings. Pressing a string down behind a fret shortens the vibrating length, changing the pitch. Each fret represents a half step in pitch, making it easier to play accurate notes and chords.

Sequence

In music, a sequence is the repetition of a set of notes at different pitch levels.

Octave

An octave is the interval between two musical notes where the higher note has twice the frequency of the lower note, creating a sense of the same pitch at different levels.

Musical alphabet

The musical alphabet refers to the sequence of letter names used to label the different pitches in Western music, spanning from A to G and repeating cyclically.

Half step /whole steps

In music, a half step is the smallest interval between two adjacent notes on a keyboard or a fretted instrument, while a whole step consists of two half steps.

Intervals

Intervals on the piano or guitar refer to the distance or relationship between two pitches, measured in terms of the number of keys or semitones between them, and are essential for understanding harmony, melody, and chord progressions.

Chromatic scale

In music, a chromatic scale is a scale consisting entirely of half steps, encompassing all twelve pitches within an octave. Practicing the chromatic scale on a guitar is beneficial for improving finger dexterity, accuracy, and familiarity with the fretboard.

Intermediate   +/- 1 hr   5 sections

3. COMPOSE
KEYS & SCALES

With the fundamentals of our instrument in place, let's move further into music theory.

This chapter focuses on the concept that forms the essence of any song: its key. You will learn how scales serve as the fundamental framework for music composition.

You will gradually grasp the intricacies of music theory and how a specific arrangement of notes can serve as a compass when crafting a song. Prepare yourself to uncover the principles that govern harmonious compositions and empower your ability to create mesmerizing melodies.

‹ WHAT YOU WILL LEARN

- The concept of key
- How to play scales
- Relative keys/scales
- Musical modes

‹ WHAT DO YOU NEED

- MIDI Keyboard
- Any 6 string guitar
- A smartphone

‹ SKIP THIS LESSON IF

- You understand key(s)
- You know major/minor scales
- You understand relative keys
- You know the modes

What is a key?

If you've ever observed musicians collaborating in a studio, you've likely encountered the question, "What key is this in?" The concept of musical key often perplexes beginners, and even experienced musicians can find it challenging to discern the key of a song. It's a topic that frequently sparks confusion and leaves many scratching their heads in search of understanding.

So let's get right into it. In music, a key refers to the primary set of pitches or notes that establish the fundamental harmonic structure of a musical composition.

Keys refer to scales

Typically, the pitches used in a song belong to a specific scale (more on this later), which determines the song's key. For instance, if a song exclusively utilizes notes from the C Major scale, it is likely to be "in the key of C Major." On your right, you'll see what this scale looks like in open position on guitar. In this case, the key lacks any sharps or flats and consists of the following notes: C-D-E-F-G-A-B-C.

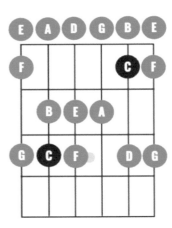

C major scale on guitar

Relative keys

In contrast, the A minor scale shares the same absence of sharps or flats. Consequently, when encountering a piece of music without any sharps or flats indicated, it could potentially be in the key of A minor as well. On the right, you'll see what the A minor scale looks like on a piano keyboard. It consists of the following notes: A-B-C-D-E-F-G-A.

A minor scale on piano

Why the key matters

Here are some key reasons.. pun intented.

Harmonic Structure

The key establishes the foundational harmonic structure of a piece of music. It provides a framework for organizing and relating different chords, melodies, and harmonies within a composition. Knowing the key allows musicians to make informed choices when creating or playing music, ensuring that the various musical elements fit together harmoniously.

Transposition

Knowledge of the key enables musicians to transpose a piece of music into a different key. Transposition is often necessary to accommodate different vocal ranges, instrument capabilities, or to suit the preferences of performers. Being able to transpose effectively relies on understanding the relationship between different keys and the corresponding adjustments needed to maintain the integrity of the original composition.

Collaboration

When collaborating with other musicians, knowing the key facilitates effective communication and understanding. It allows musicians to quickly communicate the harmonic structure and helps in coordinating their contributions. For instance, if a guitarist knows the key, they can easily play compatible chords alongside a vocalist or another instrumentalist.

Improvisation and Composition

Understanding the key opens up opportunities for improvisation and composition. Musicians can confidently explore melodies, harmonies, and chord progressions within the established key, allowing for creative expression and adding personal flair to their performances.

Compatibility

When remixing or working with acapellas, you want your new elements (instrumentals, beats, or other vocal tracks) to harmonize with the original song. Knowing the key allows you to choose musical elements that are compatible with the original, ensuring that your remix sounds coherent and pleasing to the ear.

Examples of keys in music

Here are four popular songs from different artists, each written in a specific key. The notes and chords in these songs originate from the corresponding scale indicated on the piano keyboard images. Knowing the key of a song allows you to play along and understand how the melodies and chords are created. We'll delve deeper into scales next.

Survivor - Eye Of The Tiger (C Minor natural)

Bon Jovi -You Give Love a Bad Name (C Minor natural)

Earth Wind & Fire - September (A Major)

Red Hot Chili Peppers - Californication (A Minor)

How to find the key

Having the ability to decipher the key of a musical piece is of paramount importance for any musician. This skill is especially vital for music producers who work with samples, as knowing the key of a sample opens up possibilities for enhancement. There are several methods to determine the key of a song or composition. We'll break those down for you.

By ear

Discovering the key by ear is a foundational skill in music, though it takes time to master. It involves attentive listening to your music, pinpointing the central note or chord—the tonic or root. Then, play a major or minor scale alongside your material and check if the notes harmonize with your chosen scale.

Key detection software

In our AI-powered era, an array of these tools exists. Widely embraced by DJs and producers, they are incredibly user-friendly. A simple Google search for "key detection tool" will unveil a multitude of options for you to explore and implement.

Examine the key signature

Considering the key signature is crucial, especially for those interested in classical music and sight-reading sheet music. In this approach, the arrangement of sharps and flats on different lines and spaces of the staff dictates consistent alterations to corresponding notes across octaves. Sharps raise notes, while flats lower them.

Decipher the chord progression

Exploring a song's chords can reveal its tonal foundation. Pay attention to the first and last chords—they often match the song's key. For instance, if it starts or ends with an F major chord, it likely centers around F major. In minor keys, an ending A minor chord suggests alignment with A minor.

Introduction to scales

Scales in music are sequences of specific notes arranged in a particular order, either ascending or descending, typically starting and ending on the same note, separated by an octave. For example, moving from one C to the next C above it, like playing middle C followed by the higher C, constitutes an octave, which spans eight notes in the scale.

To understand scales, think of them as the alphabet. Just as letters combine to form words and sentences in a language, scales provide the foundational notes for creating melodies, harmonies, and chord progressions in music. Each scale follows a unique pattern of intervals, which are the distances between notes. These intervals are measured in semitones (half steps) and tones (whole steps), creating the distinct character and mood of each scale.

Scale types
There are many types of scales, each with its own character. For instance, the major scale often sounds happy, while the minor scale tends to sound sad. Each scale can start on any of the 12 notes, and the scale is named after its starting note.

To construct scales on the piano and guitar, we use scale formulas, which are patterns of half steps and whole steps starting from any given note. These formulas help us memorize and play scales more easily across the fretboard.

For example, the major scale formula (W-W-H-W-W-W-H) can be applied starting from any root note, allowing you to play the scale in any key. Quick reminder that "W" means 'whole tone' and "H" means 'half tone'.

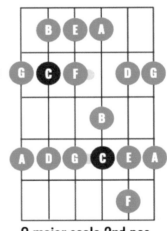

C major scale 2nd pos.

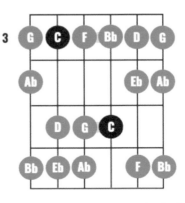

C natural minor scale 2nd pos.

Playing scales on one string

The quickest and most effective way to learn and understand scales is to start by playing them on a single string. As mentioned earlier, a scale is simply a sequence of notes separated by specific intervals. Visualizing these intervals is easiest when you limit yourself to one string. Therefore, even though scales are rarely played this way in actual practice, beginning with a single string provides a solid foundation for understanding their structure.

Let's start with the major scale, which is fundamental to music theory. The major scale is the cornerstone of all scales and serves as a reference point for understanding others. Here's how we can approach it.

Let's take the major scale as an example and play it on a single string. The sequence of intervals required to produce the major scale is as follows: Root note, whole step, whole step, half step, whole step, whole step, whole step, half step.

Think of the root note as the 'home' note or the starting point of the scale. For instance, the root note of the A major scale is 'A', the root note of the D minor scale is 'D', and the root note of the E-flat (Eb) major scale is 'Eb'.

Now, let's visually represent this interval sequence to make it more engaging:

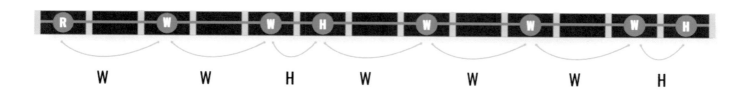

This visual approach will help you understand and internalize the structure of the major scale as you play it along a single string. Starting from the root note (e.g., A for A major), move up two frets for a whole step, another two frets for a second whole step, one fret for a half step, two frets for a whole step, another two frets for a whole step, two more frets for a third whole step, and finally one fret for the last half step.

The major scale

A scale serves as a fundamental source of notes when composing music. The notes within a scale can be rearranged in various orders, repeated as desired, and not all the notes need to be used. These notes can be performed on any instrument or sung in any musical style, adapting to different rhythms and tempos.

However, when creating music, it's not enough to simply play a scale in its original order, note by note, going up and down. Such a monotonous approach would quickly bore listeners, akin to reciting the alphabet in a conversation. To make melodies engaging, the notes within a scale must be arranged in interesting ways.

While you won't typically play a scale in its original order when writing a song, it's still beneficial to learn scales in their traditional ascending and descending patterns. This is because it helps with memorization. Just as you learned to memorize the alphabet during your early years, memorizing scale patterns in music is important. The good news is that once you understand the formula, you can effortlessly play any scale from any key!

The C major scale

Let's explore the major scale formula and see how it looks when played on a single string. Later, we'll learn how to play scales across multiple strings. Remember, a major scale can start on any note, and the formula is:

Scale formula: Whole step - Whole step - Half step - Whole step - Whole step - Whole step - Half step

Take a moment to vocalize this pattern aloud, repeating it to internalize the sequence. Now, try playing this pattern starting on the first fret of the B string, which is the C note.

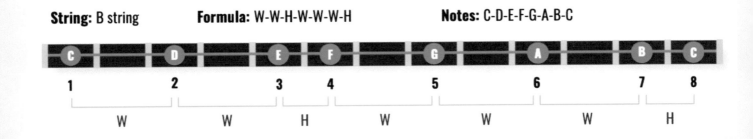

The natural minor scale

The natural minor scale is a fundamental scale in music that provides a darker, more somber sound compared to the major scale. On the guitar, it follows a specific pattern of intervals starting from the root note: whole step, half step, whole step, whole step, half step, whole step, whole step.

This scale is crucial for playing minor key music and is often used in almost any genre such as rock, metal, R&B, Hip-Hop and classical. Learning the natural minor scale in various positions on the fretboard enhances your ability to improvise and compose in minor keys.

Now, let's explore the natural minor scale on a single string. The main difference between the major and natural minor scales is that the 3rd, 6th, and 7th intervals are flattened (lowered) by a half step in the natural minor scale. This creates a darker, more somber sound compared to the major scale. Understanding the formulas for both major and natural minor scales will give you the essential knowledge to create music in both tonalities.

The C natural minor scale

We have three main types of minor scales: natural minor, harmonic minor, and melodic minor. The natural minor scale is the most common in music, so our focus will be on understanding it.

Scale formula: Whole - Half - Whole - Whole - Half - Whole - Whole

To remember this pattern, say "W - H - W - W - H - W - W" aloud to reinforce the minor scale formula in your memory. Now, try playing this pattern starting on the first fret of the B string, which is the C note.

String: B string   **Formula:** W-H-W-W-H-W-W   **Notes:** C-D-Eb-F-G-Ab-Bb-C

C		D	Eb		F		G	Ab		Bb		C
1		2	3		4		5	6		7		8

W - H - W - W - H - W - W

The major pentatonic scale

The pentatonic scale is likely the most important scale you'll learn as a guitar player. Especially if you're into soloing. This scale has been the foundation for many iconic guitar solos throughout history, making it an ideal starting point for creating your own solos.

Like most other scales, the pentatonic scale is derived from the major scale. "Penta" means five, indicating that the pentatonic scale contains only five notes. These notes are obtained by removing the fourth and seventh notes from the major scale.

This alteration removes two of the more dissonant intervals, allowing the remaining notes to be used more freely. As a result, you don't have to worry as much about landing on an "off" note while improvising and soloing.

Let's first look at the major pentatonic scale on the B string below, and then we'll explore the minor variant.

The C major pentatonic scale

We have two main types of pentatonic scales: the major pentatonic scale and the minor pentatonic scale. The formula for the major pentatonic scale is:

Scale Formula: Whole - Whole - Whole and a half - Whole - Whole and a half

To remember this pattern, you can say "W - W - WH - W - WH" aloud to reinforce the major pentatonic scale formula in your memory. Now, try playing this pattern starting on the first fret of the B string, which is the C note.

String: B string   **Formula:** W-W-WH-W-WH   **Notes:** C-D-E-G-A-C

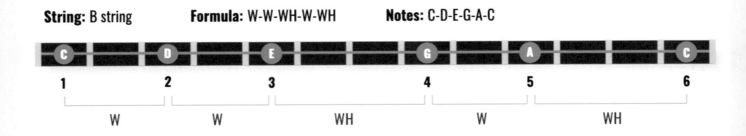

The minor pentatonic scale

The minor pentatonic scale is a fundamental scale for any guitarist. Known for its darker, bluesy, and soulful sound, it forms the backbone of countless legendary solos, making it an excellent starting point for your musical explorations.

Derived from the natural minor scale, the minor pentatonic scale consists of five notes, as "penta" means five. This scale is formed by removing the second and sixth notes from the natural minor scale.

This modification eliminates some of the more dissonant intervals, allowing the remaining notes to be used more freely. As a result, you can improvise and solo without worrying as much about hitting a wrong note.

Let's start by looking at the A minor pentatonic scale on the B string below.

The C minor pentatonic scale

We have two main types of pentatonic scales: the major pentatonic scale and the minor pentatonic scale. The formula for the minor pentatonic scale is:

Scale Formula: Whole and a half - Whole - Whole - Whole and a half - Whole

To remember this pattern, you can say "WH - W - W - WH - W" aloud to reinforce the minor pentatonic scale formula in your memory. Now, try playing this pattern starting on the first fret of the B string, which is the C note.

String: B string   **Formula:** WH-W-W-WH-W   **Notes:** C-Eb-F-G-Bb-C

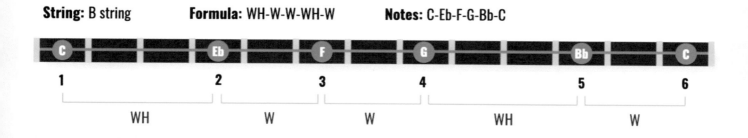

All single string scales

We've introduced you to some of the more familiar scales, but there are many other scales you can explore and practice in music theory. Below, you'll find the formulas and single-string examples for the most essential scales in music.

Scale: Blues   **Scale formula:** WH-W-H-H-WH-W   **Notes:** C-Eb-F-Gb-G-Bb-C

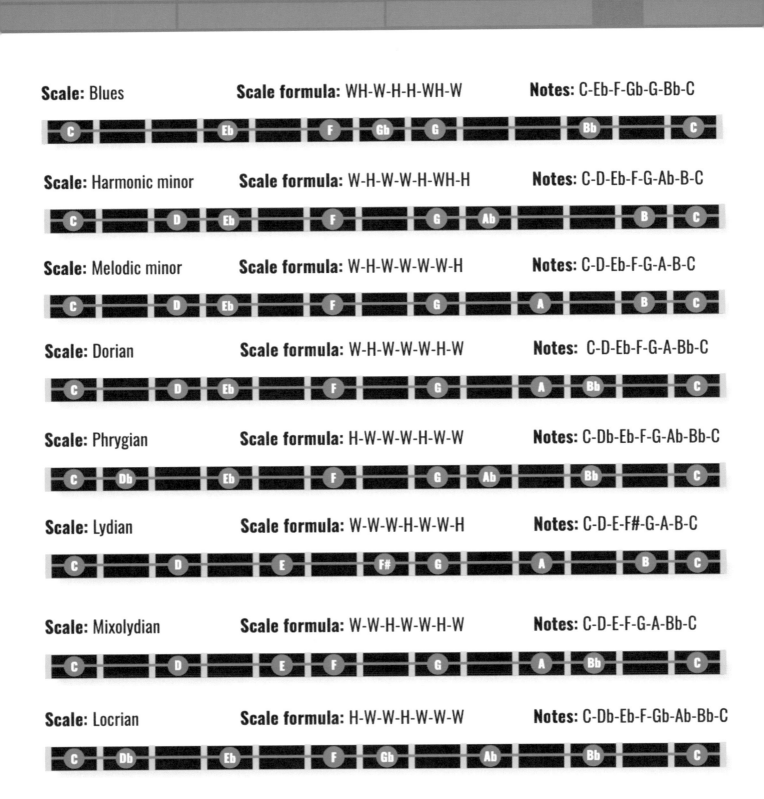

Scale: Harmonic minor   **Scale formula:** W-H-W-W-H-WH-H   **Notes:** C-D-Eb-F-G-Ab-B-C

Scale: Melodic minor   **Scale formula:** W-H-W-W-W-W-H   **Notes:** C-D-Eb-F-G-A-B-C

Scale: Dorian   **Scale formula:** W-H-W-W-W-H-W   **Notes:** C-D-Eb-F-G-A-Bb-C

Scale: Phrygian   **Scale formula:** H-W-W-W-H-W-W   **Notes:** C-Db-Eb-F-G-Ab-Bb-C

Scale: Lydian   **Scale formula:** W-W-W-H-W-W-H   **Notes:** C-D-E-F#-G-A-B-C

Scale: Mixolydian   **Scale formula:** W-W-H-W-W-H-W   **Notes:** C-D-E-F-G-A-Bb-C

Scale: Locrian   **Scale formula:** H-W-W-H-W-W-W   **Notes:** C-Db-Eb-F-Gb-Ab-Bb-C

Creating scales in different keys

One remarkable aspect of the scale formula is its versatility. Once you grasp it, you can play any scale in any key effortlessly. For instance, the formula used to construct a C Major scale can be applied starting from any note to create the corresponding major scale for that note.

The pattern of whole and half steps remains consistent. On a piano, you can simply shift all notes up a whole step to play the same pattern and form a major scale in the key of D, as shown below.

C major scale

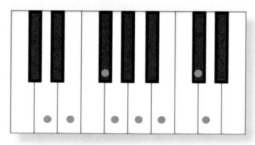

D major scale

Different keys on guitar

The same principle of movable scale patterns applies to the guitar, but with some differences due to its layout and six strings. On a guitar, there are numerous ways to play scales, allowing for patterns on two, three, four, or five strings, or even diagonally across the fretboard.

Most strings on a guitar are tuned in perfect fourths (five frets apart), except between the G and B strings, which are tuned a major third apart (four frets).

Therefore, if you're playing a scale on just the 6th and 5th strings, you can't simply copy the same pattern to the higher strings without adjustments. When moving scale patterns across the strings, you need to account for this interval difference, especially when crossing from the G string to the B string.

Scale positions

While practicing scales on a single string is an excellent method for understanding a scale's structure and intervals, it does not reflect how scales are typically used in real musical contexts. No one ever really plays a full solo on just a single string. In actual melodies and solos, scales are played in fixed positions across multiple strings, allowing for more fluid and versatile playing.

How to play scales on multiple strings
To play scales across multiple strings, you need to maintain the same pattern of whole steps and half steps. This requires familiarity with the notes on the fretboard. However, because the fretboard layout can be complex, guitarists often rely on scale patterns to simplify playing scales in any key. Begin by identifying the root note to ensure you're starting in the correct position.

For instance, if you want to play an A major scale, locate any root note, for example, the one on the 5th fret of the 6th string. From there, follow the sequence of whole steps and half steps to play the A major scale across different strings, maintaining the pattern as you move from string to string.

Movable shapes
The scale example on the right is a movable shape because it already accounts for the tuning difference between the G and B strings. This movability allows you to use the same scale shapes in different keys by simply changing the starting position, as demonstrated on the right.

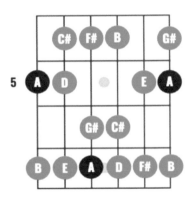

A Major scale

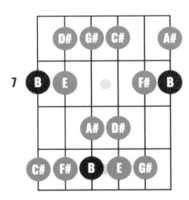

B Major scale

C major - open scale position

Now let's play scales across the fretboard using different scale positions. Let's take the C major scale as an example. By using various finger positions, we can play the C major scale in ways that limit the notes to just a few frets. This allows us to cover a smaller area of the fretboard and use multiple strings, making it easier to access all the notes in the scale efficiently.

A scale doesn't always have to start or end on its root note. On the guitar, it's important to memorize and play your scales across the entire fretboard. This approach allows you to expand the scale into multiple octaves, enhancing your playing range and versatility.

There are numerous finger positions for playing the C major scale across the fretboard, covering various octaves. We determined these positions based on the lowest fret where you can comfortably play the notes with your fretting hand. Let's take a look at some of these different scale positions, starting with the open position.

When playing the C major scale in the open position, you'll use only the first three frets and include open strings. This position uses your first three fingers: your index finger for notes on the first fret, your middle finger for notes on the second fret, and your ring finger for notes on the third fret. The diagram below shows the notes of the C major scale in this open position.

C major scale - open position

When playing the C major scale in the open position, keep your fingers confined to the first three frets. Use your index finger for notes on the first fret, your middle finger for notes on the second fret, and your ring finger for notes on the third fret.

Position: Open   **Formula:** W-W-H-W-W-W-H   **Notes:** C-D-E-F-G-A-B-C

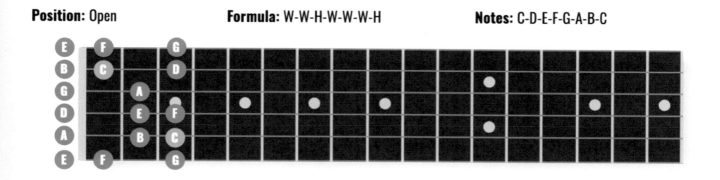

C major - Second position

Now that you can play the C major scale using open strings, let's explore the second position, starting from the third fret of the 5th string (A string). This position mainly covers the 2nd to 6th frets and uses no open strings, including notes outside the typical open position octave.

Begin with your ring finger on the third fret of the 5th string (C note), and shift your fretting hand up one fret so your index finger is on the second fret, middle finger on the third fret, ring finger on the fourth fret, and little finger on the fifth and sixth frets.

As you play through the scale, ensure each finger covers the correct frets: for example, 3rd and 5th frets on the 5th string, and 2nd, 3rd, and 5th frets on the 4th string, continuing this pattern across all strings. When you reach the 2nd (B) and 1st (high E) strings, move your hand up another fret to reach the note on the 6th fret of the 2nd string with your little finger.

This hand positioning allows for efficient movement and helps you cover a wider range of notes, making it easier to play the scale smoothly and accurately across the fretboard.

C major scale - 2nd position

When playing the C major scale in the second position, use your index finger for notes on the second fret, middle finger for the third fret, ring finger for the fourth fret, and little finger for the fifth and sixth frets.

Position: 2nd position   **Formula:** W-W-H-W-W-W-H   **Notes:** C-D-E-F-G-A-B-C

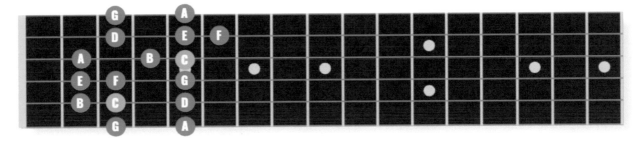

C major - Fourth position

In this position, we will play the C major scale across two octaves. The root note (C) of the first octave starts on the 8th fret of the 6th string (E) and ends on the 5th fret of the 3rd string (G). We have already played these notes in this octave in the previous two positions, but on different frets and strings using different fingers. The second octave begins on the same C note and ends on the 8th fret of the 1st string (high E), resulting in higher-pitched notes.

This position is challenging to play, but not impossible. Unlike the previous scale positions, this one requires your fretting hand to move freely rather than staying fixed.

Use your index, ring, and little fingers to play the notes on the 5th, 7th, and 8th frets on the 6th, 5th, and 4th strings. For the notes on the 3rd string, shift your fretting hand down the neck by one fret, using your pointer, middle, and little fingers to play the 4th, 5th, and 7th frets.

After that, return your hand to the original position to play the remaining notes on the 2nd and 1st strings. Below you'll see what this position looks like on the guitar fretboard. Try it out for yourself and play the scale a few times to get a feeling for it.

C major scale - 4th position

When playing the C major scale in the fourth position, use your index finger for notes on the fifth fret, middle finger for the sixth fret, ring finger for the seventh fret, and little finger for the eighth fret.

Position: 4th position   **Formula:** W-W-H-W-W-W-H   **Notes:** C-D-E-F-G-A-B-C

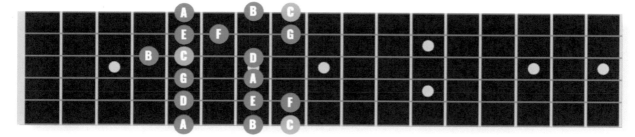

C major - Seventh position

The octaves used in this scale position are the same as those in the previous scale shape, covering the same two octaves. The key difference is that the notes on each string begin from the 7th fret, except for the notes on the 2nd string (B), which start from the 8th fret. This positioning allows you to stay within a more compact area of the fretboard.

In this position, there's no need to move the fretting hand back and forth across the neck, making it easier to play quickly and accurately. All the notes are close together and easily accessible, which helps in maintaining a smooth and consistent playing technique. Use your index finger for notes on the 7th fret, middle finger for notes on the 8th fret, ring finger for notes on the 9th fret, and little finger for notes on the 10th fret.

This efficient finger placement not only makes it easier to play the scale but also aids in transitioning between notes smoothly. This positioning is particularly useful for faster passages and for maintaining clarity in your playing. The following tablature illustrates this position clearly, highlighting the finger placement and the notes to be played.

C major scale - 7th position

When playing the C major scale in the seventh position, use your index finger for notes on the seventh fret, middle finger for the eighth fret, ring finger for the ninth fret, and little finger for the tenth fret.

Position: 7th position   **Formula:** W-W-H-W-W-W-H   **Notes:** C-D-E-F-G-A-B-C

C major - Eighth position

For this position, start by playing from the root note C on the 8th fret of the low E string. This position covers the same notes across two octaves as the previous scale shapes but uses different frets and strings. Therefore, it is crucial to use the correct fingers to access these notes effectively.

This position involves some stretching. You will need to stretch your fretting hand slightly to use your little finger for notes on the 12th fret. For the notes on the 2nd (B) and 1st (high E) strings, you should position your fretting hand higher up the neck to allow your ring and little fingers to access the notes on the 12th frets.

Using the correct finger positioning ensures better access and control over the notes. Remember to keep your hand relaxed and practice slowly at first, ensuring accuracy before gradually increasing speed. This will help you master the stretches and transitions needed to play the scale smoothly in this position.

Below you'll see a diagram of this scale position. Try it out for yourself and play the scale a few times to get a feeling for it.

C major scale - 8th position

When playing the C major scale in this position, start from the root note C on the 8th fret of the low E string. Use your index finger for notes on the 8th fret, middle finger for notes on the 9th fret, ring finger for notes on the 10th fret, and little finger for notes on the 12th fret.

Position: 8th position　　**Formula:** W-W-H-W-W-W-H　　**Notes:** C-D-E-F-G-A-B-C

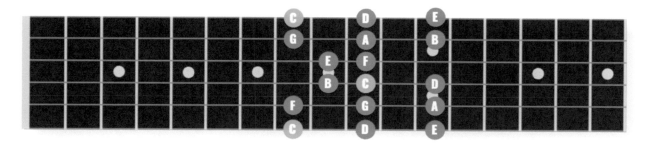

C major - Twelfth position

This is the final position in the C major scale, incorporating notes from a much higher octave that we haven't yet explored. Playing notes on the 12th, 13th, 14th, and 15th frets results in a significantly higher pitch, giving the scale a bright and distinct sound.

Despite dealing with higher octaves, playing these notes typically requires less stretching of the fretting hand due to the smaller distance between the higher frets. However, the action of the strings can still make it challenging to play these notes cleanly without buzzing. It's important to press down firmly and accurately to avoid any unwanted noise.

In this position, the compact nature of the higher frets allows for faster playing, making it ideal for solos and high-speed passages. As with the other scale positions, using the appropriate fingers of your fretting hand is essential for accuracy and ease of play. Proper finger placement will help you navigate the higher frets with confidence and precision.

Below you'll see a diagram of this scale position. Try it out for yourself and play the scale a few times to get a feeling for it.

C major scale - 12th position

When playing the C major scale in this higher position, use your index finger for notes on the 12th fret, middle finger for the 13th fret, ring finger for the 14th fret, and little finger for the 15th fret. This finger placement ensures smooth navigation of the higher frets.

Position: 12th position   **Formula:** W-W-H-W-W-W-H   **Notes:** C-D-E-F-G-A-B-C

C Major scale on whole fretboard

One effective way to visualize where you can play the C major scale (or any other scale in the key of C) is by knowing where all the root notes and corresponding scale notes are located on your guitar fretboard. By identifying all the C notes, you can map out the rest of the C major scale around these root notes.

First, start by marking all the C notes on the fretboard. These are your root notes and will serve as the foundation for mapping out the rest of the scale. Next, fill in the other notes of the C major scale (D, E, F, G, A, B) around each C note within the surrounding frets. This helps in creating a mental map of where all the scale notes are in relation to the root notes.

By understanding where the C notes are, you can use these reference points to find and play the C major scale anywhere on the fretboard. This approach provides a clear road-map, making it easier to navigate the fretboard and play the scale in various positions and octaves.

For example, you can identify the C notes on the 6th string (8th fret), 5th string (3rd and 15th frets), 4th string (10th fret), 3rd string (5th and 17th frets), 2nd string (1st and 13th fret), and 1st string (8th fret).

Then, fill in the surrounding scale notes: around the C note on the 8th fret of the 6th string, you have D (10th fret), E (12th fret), F (13th fret), G (10th fret on the 5th string), A (12th fret on the 5th string), and B (14th fret on the 5th string).

By systematically marking the C notes and filling in the surrounding scale notes, you can effectively visualize and play the C major scale across the entire fretboard. This method not only aids in learning scales but also enhances your overall understanding of the guitar fretboard, making it easier to navigate and improvise in any key.

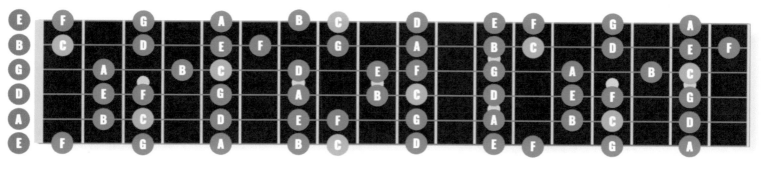

Scale systems

To play scales on the guitar, there are numerous systems to help you map out the fretboard. While it is helpful to learn all of them, what's most important is to practice playing scales starting from any note on the neck using each finger. This approach will naturally help you learn and adapt to most systems. The ultimate goal of learning scales is to internalize all intervals and develop muscle memory for moving between them.

A highly effective method is to play major scales from any note and sing along. Singing the scales, both with and without the instrument, trains your ear and helps you connect your auditory perception with your finger movements. If you know what a scale sounds like, all you have to do is find any root note and you'll be able to quickly play the scale.

In this book, we won't cover all the systems, but we will focus on the CAGED system, which offers some additional benefits. Here are some of the most commonly used systems for playing scales on the guitar.

CAGED System
The CAGED system divides the guitar fretboard into five shapes based on open chord forms: C, A, G, E, and D. These shapes help you visualize and connect major chords and scales across the neck, making it easier to understand the layout of the fretboard and transition between chords and scales.

3-Note-Per-String System
This system involves playing three notes on each string, which facilitates smooth and efficient picking. It is particularly useful for playing scales quickly and fluidly, making it a popular choice for fast soloing and scale practice.

4-Note-Per-String System
This less common system involves playing four notes per string. It is useful for certain extended scales and modes, promoting finger independence and stretching. This method can be helpful for advanced players looking to explore wider intervals and complex musical ideas.

Box Patterns
Box patterns are fixed shapes that span four or five frets, often used for pentatonic and blues scales. These patterns are easy to memorize and allow for quick position shifts, making them ideal for soloing in blues and rock music.

Relative keys

Relative scales are major and minor scales that share the same notes, chords, and key signature. Every major scale has a relative minor scale, and every minor scale has a relative major scale. The relative minor scale of any major scale is always found at the 6th degree of the major scale. To determine the relative minor, list the notes of the major scale and identify the 6th note. This note serves as the root of the relative minor scale.

To find the relative minor of C major, we need to list the notes of the C major scale. The 6th degree of the C major scale is A, which means A minor is the relative minor of C major.

By following the same pattern of whole steps and half steps for the minor scale, we find that the notes of the A minor scale are exactly the same as those of the C major scale.

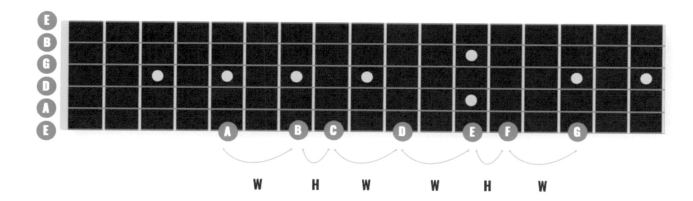

Side by side

Placing two-octave scale patterns for both C major and A minor side by side highlights this clearly: both scales share the same seven notes. The only difference is the root note upon which each scale is built. These two keys not only share the same notes but also the same chords. We'll delve deeper into this later.

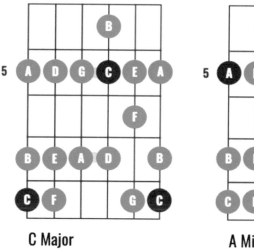

C Major

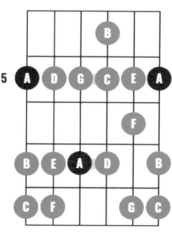

A Minor

Relative keys

Another way to determine the relative minor key of a given major key is to move down three half steps/semitones, or a minor third, from the tonic note of the major scale. On the guitar, this can be easily visualized by locating the tonic note on any string and moving three frets down.

For example, in C major, its relative minor is A minor. In the image on the right, we count down three half steps to get to the relative minor. Understanding relative minors connects major and minor keys, expanding your musical options. On the table below you can see how you can find the relative minor scale on piano. The same applies to guitar.

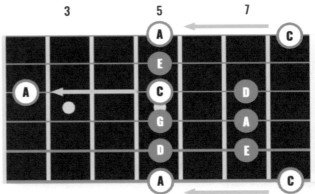

3 half steps down

Major key	Relative minor	Tonic (first note)	6th up	Relative minor
C Major	A Minor		→	
Db Major	Bb Minor		→	
D Major	B Minor		→	
Eb Major	C Minor		→	
E Major	C# Minor		→	
F Major	D Minor		→	
F# Major	D# Minor		→	
G Major	E Minor		→	
Ab Major	F Minor		→	
A Major	F# Minor		→	
Bb Major	G Minor		→	
B Major	G# Minor		→	

How to use relative scales

The relative minor of a major key has the same key signature, meaning it has the same number of sharps or flats. The difference lies in which note serves as the tonic or starting point. For example, the relative minor of C major is A minor, and both have no sharps or flats in their key signature. Similarly, the relative minor of G major is E minor, and both have one sharp in their key signature (F#).

See for yourself

To the right, you'll find C major and its relative A minor, as well as G major and its relative E minor. Notice both A and C have no sharps or flats, while G and E both have one sharp key.

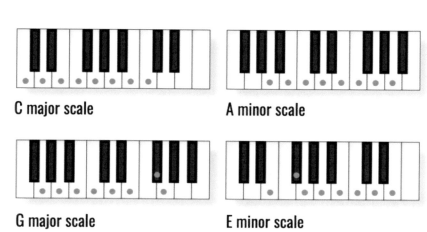

C major scale

A minor scale

G major scale

E minor scale

Shift the mood

Switching between a major and its relative minor can alter the emotional tone of your song. For example, transitioning from C major to its relative A minor can introduce a more melancholic or introspective feel.

Smooth transitions

Moving between relative keys can provide seamless transitions between sections of your song. This is beneficial when changing from a bright major section to a more subdued minor section.

Parallel chord progressions

Experiment with parallel chord progressions that use chords from both the major and relative minor keys. This can add harmonic richness and unpredictability to your music.

Key changes

Transitioning from one relative key to another can act as a subtle key change within a piece of music. This can be a creative way to introduce diversity while maintaining a thematic connection.

The musical modes

Modes in music offer flexibility by starting on different scale degrees rather than the root note. They're like unique patterns created from the same set of notes, much like building various structures from a set of blocks. These structures, or modes, possess distinct shapes and characters, all originating from the major scale, serving as your fundamental building blocks.

Ionian Mode
It's the 'do re mi' major key, the modern major scale starting on C with natural notes.

W-W-H-W-W-H

Dorian Mode
Resembles the natural minor scale, differing in the sixth note—it's a major sixth above the first.

W-H-W-W-W-H-W

Phrygian Mode
Similar to the natural minor scale, but distinguished by its unique minor second. The interval between the root and the second note is a minor second, or a half step, giving it a distinct sound.

H-W-W-W-H-W-W

Lydian Mode
Differs from the Ionian (major scale) by sharpening the fourth note, creating a subtly dreamy, magical sound.

W-W-W-H-W-W-H

Mixolydian Mode
Set apart from the major scale by its flattened seventh note, as opposed to the major seventh.

W-W-H-W-W-H-W

Aeolian Mode
Essentially the natural minor scale, featured in popular songs like Bob Dylan's 'All along the watchtower' and REM's 'Losing my Religion.

W-H-W-W-H-W-W

Locrian Mode
Considered the darkest and least stable of all modes due to the presence of a diminished fifth and lowered second and seventh degrees.

H-W-W-H-W-W-W

How to use the modes

Modes are like different flavors of ice cream. Just as vanilla and chocolate taste different, modes make music sound distinct too. Each mode is a special sequence of notes with its own unique feelings and mood.

Now, we won't go too deep into modes, because you might not use them all the time. It's a bit like having lots of ice cream flavors, but you don't eat them every day. But it's still good to know about them because one day, you might want to try a new flavor in your music, and knowing about modes can help you do that.

First, you can pick a mode to create the mood of your music. It's like choosing the colors for a painting. Each mode gives your music a different feeling.

You can also mix and match modes to make your music sound interesting and unique. It's a bit like mixing flavors to create a new and exciting ice cream.

And if you want to be really creative, you can use modes that are a bit different from the usual ones. This is like trying new and surprising things in your music.

In short, modes are musical tools that help you make your own special tunes with different feelings, surprises, and flavors!

Mode name	Interval sequence	Formula	Example
Ionian	W-W-H-W-W-W-H	1-2-3-4-5-6-7	
Dorian	W-H-W-W-W-H-W	1-2-b3-4-5-6-b7	
Phrygian	H-W-W-W-H-W-W	1-b2-b3-4-5-b6-b7	
Lydian	W-W-W-H-W-W-H	1-2-3-#4-5-6-7	
Mixolydian	W-W-H-W-W-H-W	1-2-3-4-5-6-b7	
Aeolian	W-H-W-W-H-W-W	1-2-b3-4-5-b6-b7	
Locrian	H-W-W-H-W-W-W	1-b2-b3-4-b5-b6-b7	

Modes chart

This guitar modes fretboard chart displays all the essential modes, mapped out across the fretboard, helping you master modal playing and expand your improvisation skills.

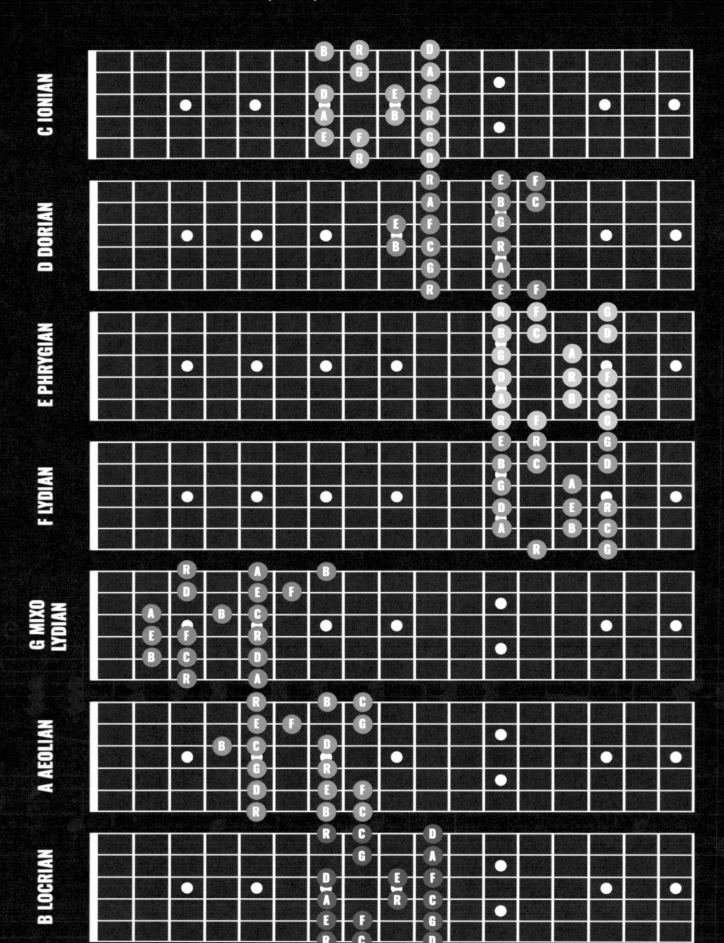

Key takeaways

In this lesson, we explored the significance of the key in determining suitable scales for your songs. By understanding the concept of scales and their formation through patterns of whole steps and half steps, we delved into the relationship between major and minor scales.

As we progress further into music theory, the complexity can increase. If you ever feel overwhelmed, it's crucial to pause, review each lesson carefully, and ensure a solid understanding before moving on to the next topic. Taking this approach will help you navigate the subject effectively and avoid confusion.

Song key

Just as choosing the right colors and crayons is important in creating a drawing, the key of a song determines the specific set of notes and chords that harmonize well together, acting as a musical palette where chords and notes must be carefully selected to fit within the song's key.

Scales

Scales in music are like magical ladders guiding us to play or sing notes in a specific order, ensuring the right notes are used in a song, while also shaping its unique mood and feeling. These patterns can be applied to any key on the keyboard, allowing us to explore a world of musical possibilities.

Relative scale

Relative scales are sets of notes that share a close musical connection, with one scale sounding happy and the other scale sounding sad, yet both scales using the same set of notes. Knowing relative scales helps you understand different moods in music and lets you create a variety of feelings in your own songs.

Musical modes

Modes are a set of scales derived from a parent scale, each with a unique pattern of intervals, used to create various tonal flavors and moods in music.

Full fretboard scales

While there are countless scales in music, mastering all of them isn't essential. Instead, focus on the most important scales listed below. We've provided these scales mapped out on the full fretboard in the key of C for your convenience. Practice these scales diligently until they become second nature. Aim to internalize the unique sound of each scale, enabling you to effortlessly apply the same scale patterns in any key.

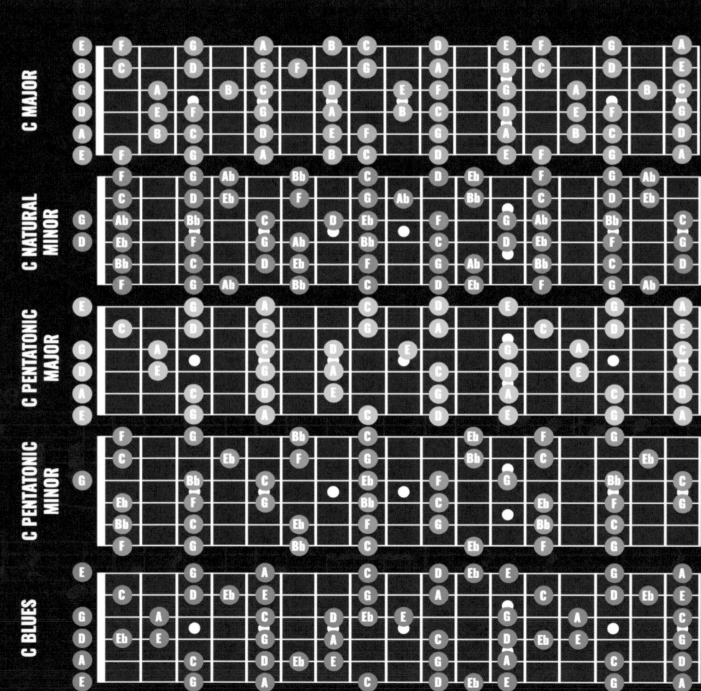

Full fretboard scales

While there are countless scales in music, mastering all of them isn't essential. Instead, focus on the most important scales listed below. We've provided these scales mapped out on the full fretboard in the key of C for your convenience. Practice these scales diligently until they become second nature. Aim to internalize the unique sound of each scale, enabling you to effortlessly apply the same scale patterns in any key.

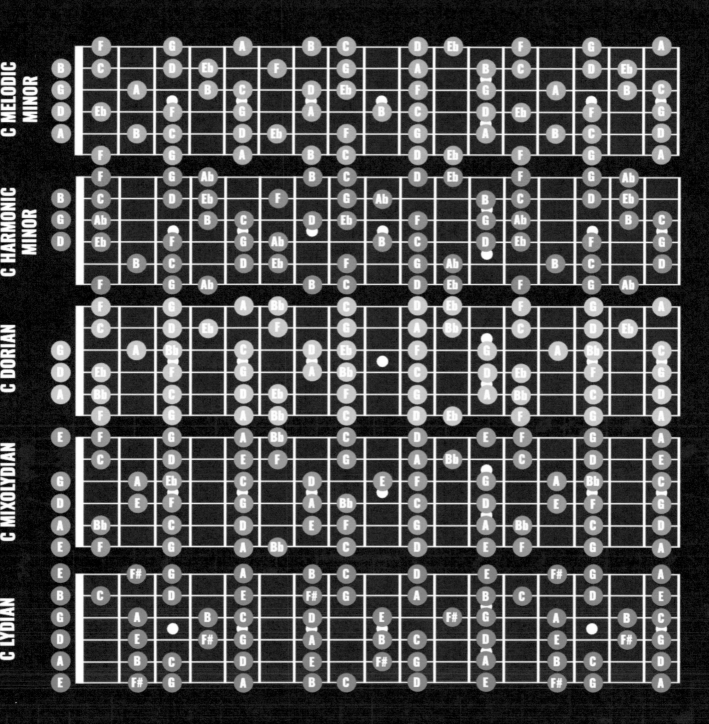

Jargon guide

Music theory can be a complex subject, and even more so with its specialized vocabulary. This guide is here to assist you in comprehending and defining the terms you've come across in this chapter or to refresh your memory.

Key

In music, a key refers to a specific set of notes or pitches within an octave that form the foundation for a musical piece. It includes a tonic note and a related scale, such as a major or minor scale. The key determines the overall sound and tonal center of the music, influencing the choice of notes and chords used in a composition.

Transposing

Transposing in music refers to the process of changing the pitch of a musical piece or a musical instrument. This can involve shifting all the notes or chords up or down by a certain interval, which can result in a higher or lower key. Transposing is often used to accommodate different instruments or vocal ranges or to make a song easier to play or sing.

Key signature

A key signature in music notation is a set of sharps (#) or flats (b) placed at the beginning of a musical staff, right after the clef symbol. It indicates the specific notes within a key and informs the musician which notes are to be consistently raised or lowered throughout the piece.

Tonic

The tonic refers to the first note or pitch of a musical scale. It serves as the central or home pitch around which a piece of music revolves. The tonic is often used as a point of reference for melodies and harmonies.

Scale formula

A scale formula in music is a specific pattern of intervals that defines a particular scale. It indicates the sequence of whole steps (W) and half steps (H) between the notes in the scale. For example, the formula for a major scale is W-W-H-W-W-W-H, where W represents a whole step and H represents a half step.

Major scale

The major scale is a seven-note scale with a specific pattern of intervals (W-W-H-W-W-W-H) that creates a bright and happy sound, serving as a fundamental building block in Western music.

Minor scale

The minor scale is a seven-note scale with a distinct pattern of intervals (W-H-W-W-H-W-W) that imparts a somber or melancholic feel and is widely used in Western music.

Relative keys

Relative keys are pairs of major and minor keys that share the same key signature. They have a close musical relationship, with one being major and the other being its relative minor. These key pairs have the same notes but start on different tonics, creating different emotional qualities in the music.

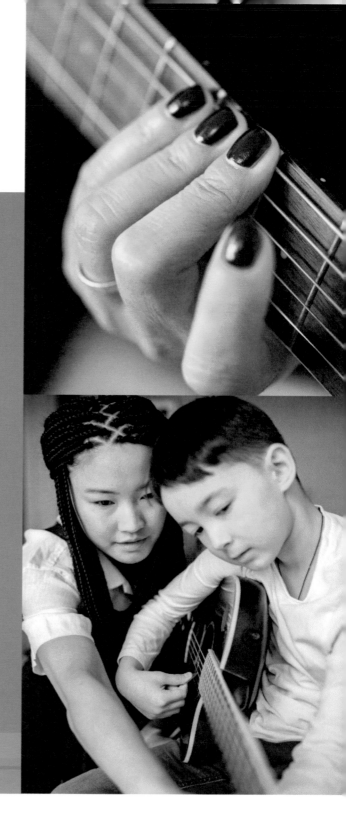

4. HARMONY
GUIDE TO CHORDS

Now that you have a solid grasp of the concept of keys and how scales are formed, it's time to take the next step and dive into the world of chords and harmony in music.

In this chapter, we will explore the core elements that give music its depth and richness, delving into the fundamental building blocks of harmony. This chapter will teach you what makes up chords, how they are constructed, and how you can alter their sound to make them sound even better and easier to play.

After this chapter you'll be able to play chords in any key and apply chord inversions.

‹ WHAT YOU WILL LEARN

- Musical intervals
- How to construct chords
- Chord types
- Chord formulas
- Transposing chords
- Chord inversions/voicings

‹ WHAT DO YOU NEED

- Any six string guitar
- Piano/MIDI Keyboard
- A smartphone

‹ SKIP THIS LESSON IF

- You know all chord formulas
- You understand intervals
- You can invert your chords
- You can transpose chords

Music intervals

Before we continue, it's essential to grasp the notion of music intervals. While we've previously covered intervals on the guitar, which denote the separation between two notes or pitches measured in semitones, some intervals encompass more than just a step or two. These intervals possess distinct names. When two pitches are identical, they are referred to as a unison. When played by the same instrument and correctly tuned, they can create the illusion of a single note.

Scale intervals play a vital role in the construction and understanding of chords and melodies. They also help us to train our ears to recognize the feeling of sounds. Chords are formed by combining multiple notes played simultaneously, and the specific intervals between these notes determine the quality and character of the chord.

Intervals are defined by a quality and a number. The number specifies the distance between two notes, including the starting note.

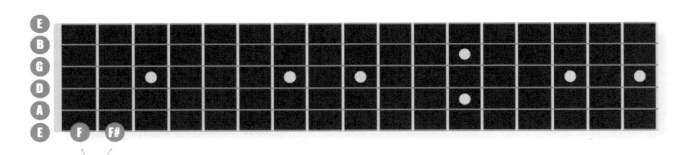

Half step (Minor 2nd)

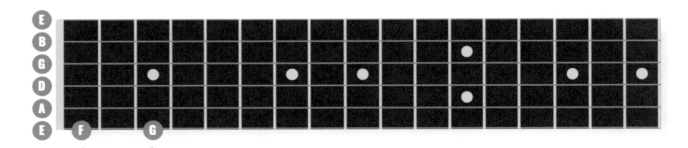

Whole step (Major 2nd)

Melodic vs harmonic

Intervals are like the essential building blocks of music. They help us understand how notes relate to each other in scales, chords, and melodies. Intervals measure the distance between two pitches, whether we hear them together at the same time (harmonic intervals) or one after the other (melodic intervals).

When we talk about harmonic intervals, we're looking at how two notes sound when played simultaneously. It's like listening to two voices singing different notes at once. We use harmonic intervals to create chords and harmonies, which give music its rich and layered sound.

On the other hand, melodic intervals focus on how notes follow each other in a sequence, like musical steps. It's like hearing a melody being played or sung, where each note leads to the next. Melodic intervals help us construct melodies, which are the catchy tunes and memorable parts of a song.

Harmonic intervals

For example, if we were to play these three notes C-E-G, we would create the C Major chord (see left image). If we were to play them in a sequence, we would create a simple melody in the key of C (see right image).

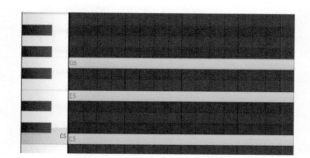

Harmonic intervals

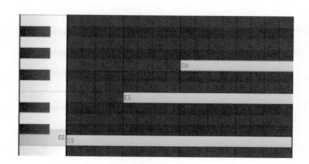

Melodic intervals

Certain intervals have specific classifications based on their qualities. Let's explore these classifications.

Interval qualities

Intervals are comprised of a number and a quality. Each interval has a unique number associated with it. For example, an interval that spans two letter names or steps is called a "second." If it spans three letter names or steps, it's called a "third," and so on.

Perfect Intervals

Perfect intervals, such as unisons, fourths, fifths, and octaves, have a stable sound and don't have major or minor classifications. They usually retain their natural, sharp, or flat qualities, except for B to F and B to F#, or Bb to F where specific alterations occur.

Perfect 4th
Consonance

Perfect 5th
Consonance

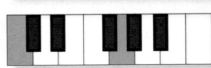

Major or Minor Intervals

Intervals such as the second, third, sixth, and seventh can be classified as major or minor intervals. These intervals can vary in their qualities, creating different moods and sounds.

Major 2nd
Dissonance

Minor 2nd
Dissonance

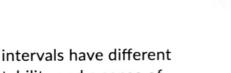

It's important to note that the perfect intervals and major/minor intervals have different characteristics and roles in music. The perfect intervals provide stability and a sense of resolution, while the major/minor intervals contribute to the expressive and emotional aspects of melodies and harmonies.

By understanding these interval classifications, musicians can accurately identify and describe the qualities of different intervals, allowing for more precise communication and analysis in music theory and practice.

Examples of intervals

To recognize intervals, link them to familiar songs. For instance, Amazing Grace starts with a perfect fourth. When you hear a similar interval, like the first two notes of that song, you'll instantly know it's a perfect fourth. Here some examples of intervals used in popular songs. Use the QR codes to navigate to the section of the song where the interval is heard.

Star Wars - Theme Song (Perfect 4th)

The Simpsons - Intro (Tritone)

Michael Jackson - Bad (Minor 3rd)

A-Ha - Take On Me (Major 7th)

How intervals are used

Here are several ways you can incorporate intervals into your music and make use of their musical properties

Melodies

Major and minor intervals play a vital role in shaping melodies. Major intervals tend to create a bright and uplifting sound, while minor intervals evoke a more melancholic or introspective mood. You can use major intervals to create joyful and uplifting melodies, while minor intervals can add a touch of emotional depth or melancholy to your melodies.

Harmonizing

Major and minor intervals are commonly used to harmonize melodies. By adding major or minor intervals above or below a melody note, you can create harmonies that enhance and support the melody. Experiment with different major and minor intervals to find harmonies that complement the emotional content and overall atmosphere of the melody.

Chord progressions

Major and minor intervals are the building blocks of chord progressions. Major intervals are linked to major chords, offering a stable sound, while minor intervals are used in minor chords to create tension or melancholy. Mixing both adds variety and depth.

Modulation and key changes

Major and minor intervals are crucial for modulating or changing keys within a musical piece. Modulating to a different key involves using intervals that shift the tonal center and create a new musical landscape. Major and minor intervals are used to establish the new tonal center and navigate the transition between keys.

Adding flavor

Major and minor intervals can be used as expressive ornaments within melodies. Adding slight variations, such as bending or sliding to a major or minor interval, can add color and emotion to your melodies. These ornaments can create subtle nuances and make your melodies more expressive and engaging.

Remember, major and minor intervals are tools for conveying emotion, creating harmony, and shaping musical expression. Experiment with different combinations, progressions, and variations to find the sound and mood that resonates with your musical vision.

Intervals on one string

On the guitar, there are various ways to play intervals. With six strings at our disposal, we can create intervals on a single string or across multiple strings. Let's begin by exploring how these intervals appear on the B string.

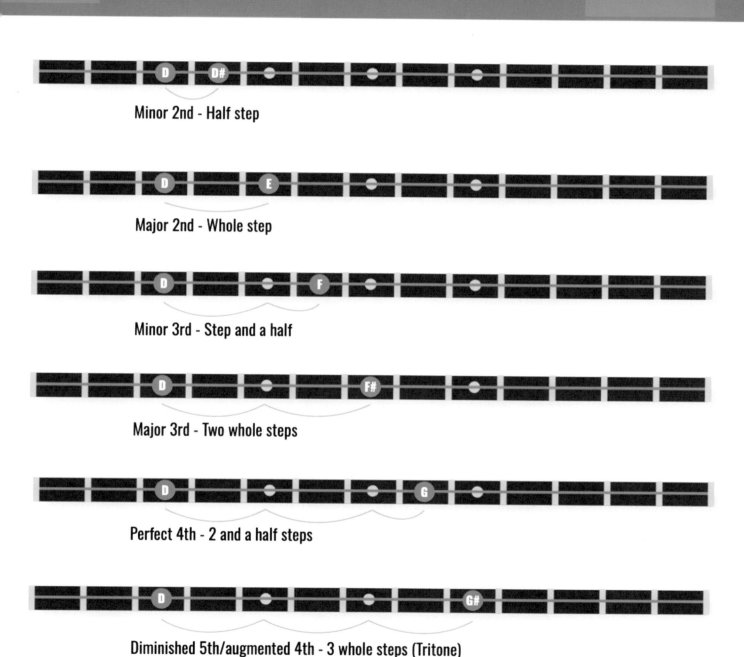

Minor 2nd - Half step

Major 2nd - Whole step

Minor 3rd - Step and a half

Major 3rd - Two whole steps

Perfect 4th - 2 and a half steps

Diminished 5th/augmented 4th - 3 whole steps (Tritone)

Perfect fifth - 3 and a half steps

Intervals on one string

On the guitar, there are various ways to play intervals. With six strings at our disposal, we can create intervals on a single string or across multiple strings. Let's begin by exploring how these intervals appear on a single string.

When we reach the interval of 6 whole steps on one string it creates an octave, meaning we've reached the same note as our starting note, but one octave higher.

These intervals form the foundation of chords and melodies. See them below and try them out on your guitar. Up next, we're gonna explore the intervals between the strings of your guitar.

Augmented 5th (#5) or minor 6th (b6) - 4 Whole Steps

Major 6th (6) or diminished 7th (bb7) - 4 and a Half Steps

Minor 7th - 5 Whole Steps

Major 7th (7) - 5 and A Half Steps

Octave (8) - 6 whole steps (12 frets)

String intervals

A guitar features six strings, each meticulously tuned to a distinct note. Transitioning from one string to another creates a musical interval, enriching the harmonic complexity and enabling a diverse range of chords and melodies. Understanding these intervals is crucial, as it enhances your grasp of the guitar's musical potential. Let's delve into the specific intervals between the guitar strings.

E to A

The interval between the low E string (6th string) and the A string (5th string) on a guitar is a perfect fourth. This interval spans five half steps or frets on the guitar.

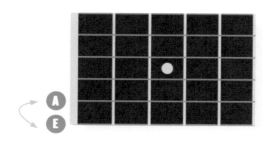

A to D

The interval between the A string (5th string) and the D string (4th string) on a guitar is also a perfect fourth. This interval spans five half steps or frets on the guitar.

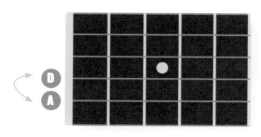

D to G

The interval between the D string (4th string) and the G string (3rd string) on a guitar is also a perfect fourth. This interval spans five half steps or frets on the guitar.

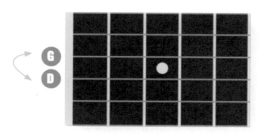

String intervals

G to B

The interval between the G string (3rd string) and the B string (2nd string) is a major third. This interval spans two whole steps. This unique interval is designed to facilitate more comfortable and practical finger positioning for chord shapes and scale patterns. By using a major third between the G and B strings, many common chord shapes, such as major and minor triads, become more manageable to play.

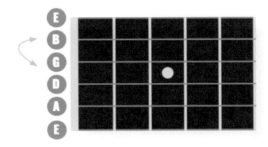

B to E

The interval between the B string (2nd string) and the high E string (1st string) on a guitar is a perfect fourth. This interval spans five half steps or frets on the guitar.

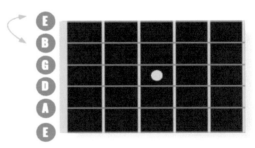

In short

In summary, the perfect fourth intervals (E to A, A to D, D to G, B to E) provide consistent spacing that simplifies the formation of scales and chord shapes across the fretboard. This regularity aids in developing muscle memory, making transitions between chords and scales smoother.

The major third interval (G to B) introduces a slight variation, facilitating more comfortable and practical finger positioning for common chord voicings and scale patterns. This deviation reduces hand stretching, enhancing the guitar's ergonomic design. Now that you're familiar with the intervals in standard tuning, let's explore more guitar intervals between the strings.

Intervals between strings

Minor 2nd

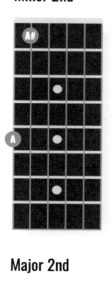 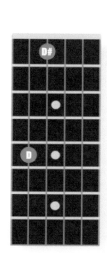 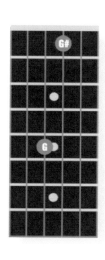 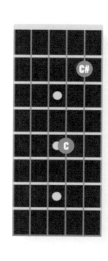 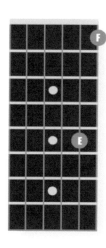

Major 2nd

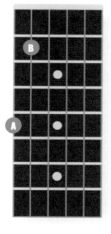 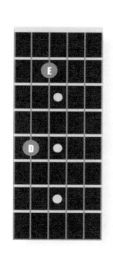 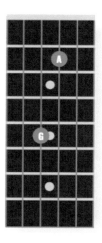 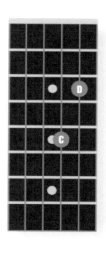 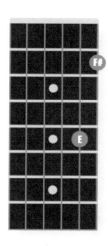

Minor 3rd

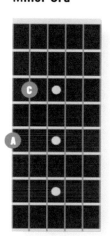 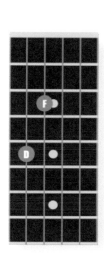 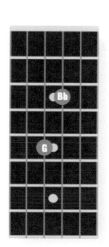 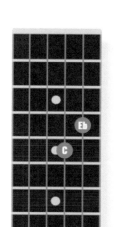 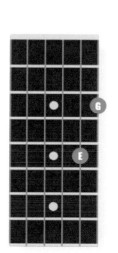

Intervals between strings

Major 3rd

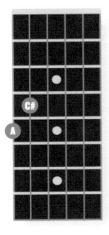 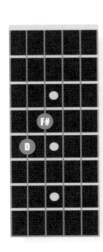 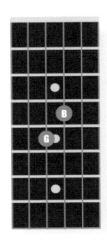 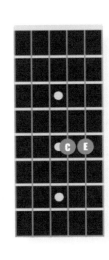 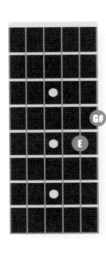

Perfect 4th

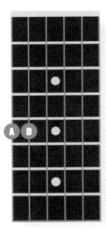 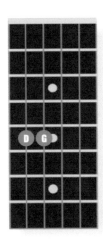 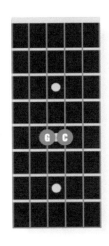 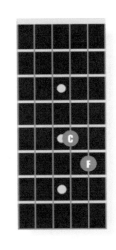 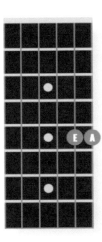

Diminished 5 or augmented 4th (Tritone)

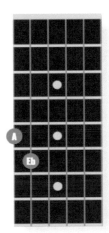 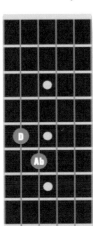 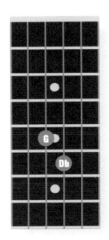 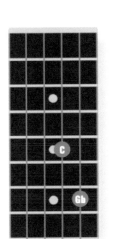 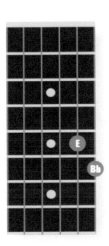

Intervals between strings

Perfect 5th

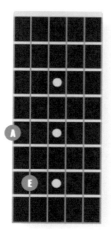 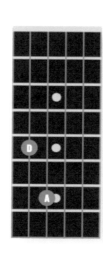 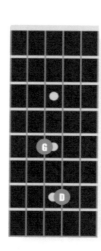 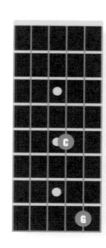 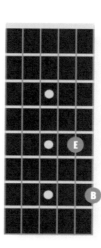

Perfect 5th (Second option)

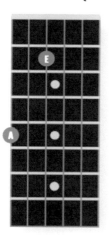 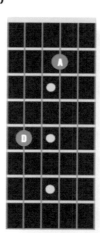 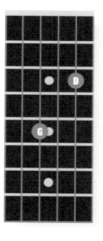 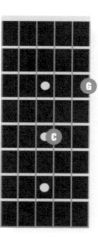

Augmented 5th or minor 6th

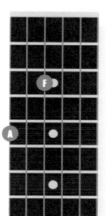 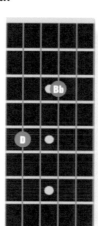 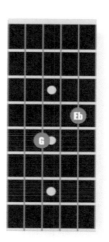 

Intervals between strings

Augmented 5th (#5) or minor 6th (b6) Option 2

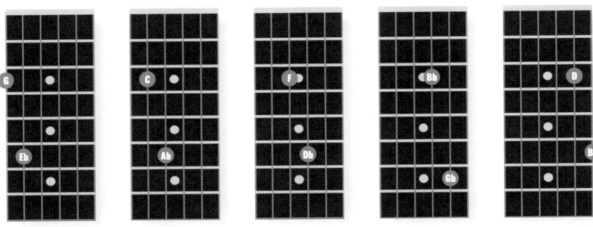

Major 6th (6) or diminished 7th (bb7)

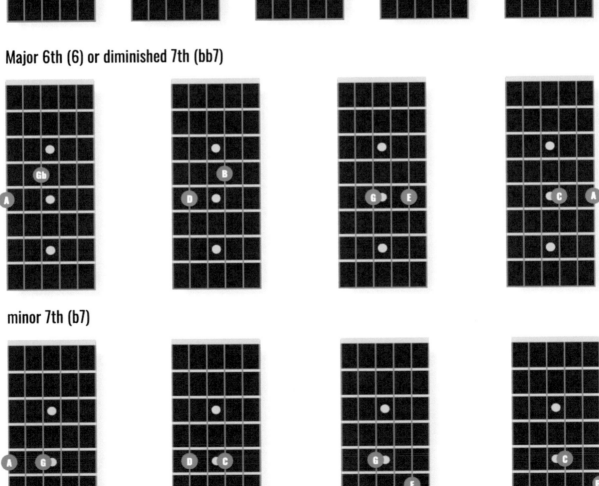

minor 7th (b7)

Intervals between strings

Major 7th

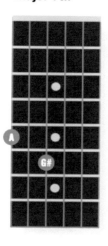 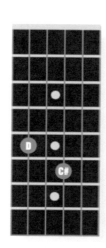 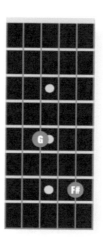 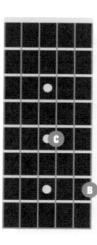

Octave (8)

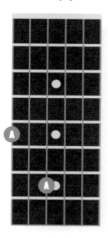 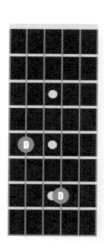 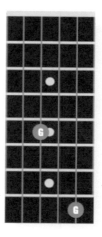 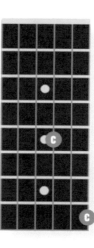

Octave (8) Option 2

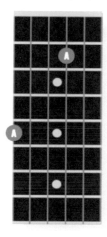 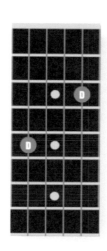 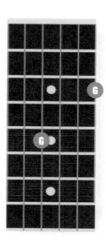

Octave shapes

Octave shape 1
(6th string)

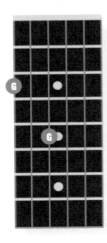

Octave shape 2
(5th string)

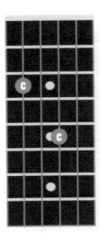

Octave shape 3
(4th string)

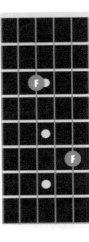

Octave shape 4
(2nd string)

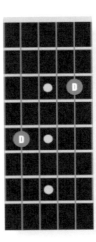

Octave shape 5
(1st string)

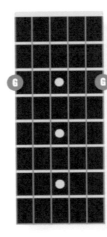

Octave shapes

All F notes using octave shapes

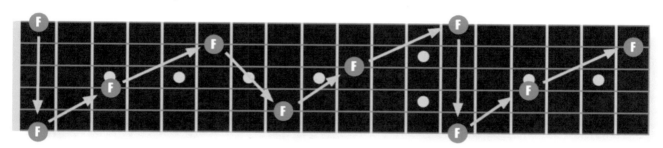

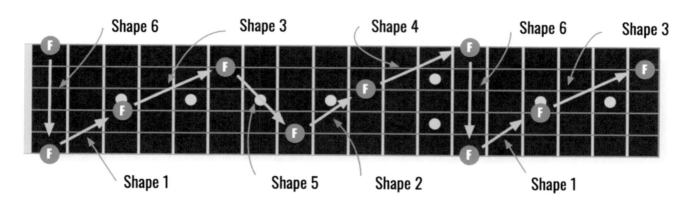

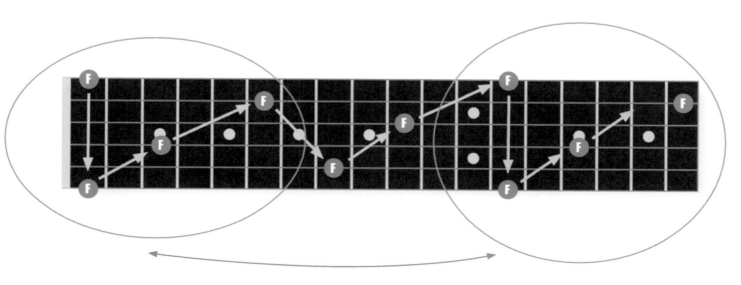

Repeats an octave higher (12 frets)

Unison note shapes

Unison shape 1
(6th/5th string)

Unison shape 2
(5th/4th string)

Unison shape 3
(4th/3rd string)

Unison shape 4
(3rd/2nd string)

Unison shape 5
(2nd/1st string)

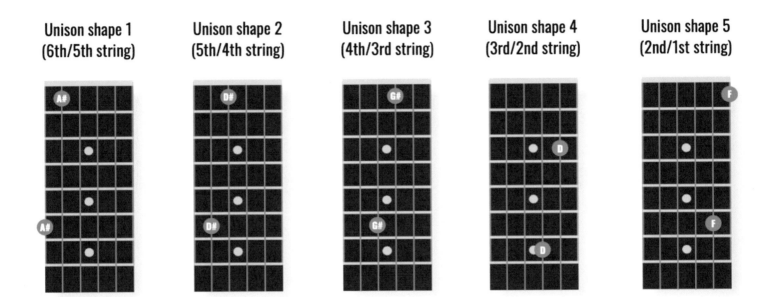

All F notes using unison note shapes

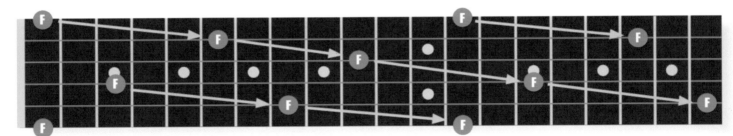

In short

Intervals on the guitar refer to the distance between two notes, either on different strings or the same string. Mastering these intervals is key to understanding music theory, improving fretboard navigation, and enhancing overall playing skills.

With this knowledge of intervals, it's time to apply it to chord construction. In the next lesson, we'll learn how to create and play various chord shapes on the guitar. Understanding how intervals form chords will help you transition smoothly and improve your playing technique and musical expression. Let's dive into chords and unlock your guitar's full potential!

Introduction to chords

A chord is a number of musical notes that sound good when played together at the same time. The notes are selected from a musical scale. There are different types of chords, each having its own unique sound and feeling. For example, major chords sound happy, minor chords sound a bit sad, and diminished chords sound tense.

Chords are built around a main note called the "root note." So, if someone says it's a C chord, that means the main note or root of the chord is always "C." While chords can be made with just two notes (power chords), most chords have at least three notes (triads) or more (seventh and extended chords).

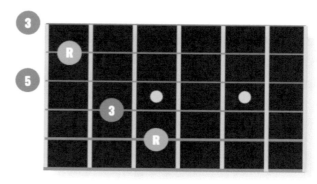

C major chord

The quality or type of a chord is determined by its scale and the specific intervals between the notes it contains. This quality gives the chord its distinct sound and feeling. For example, a major chord has a bright and happy sound, while a minor chord has a more somber and sad quality.

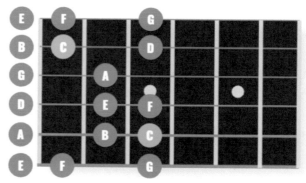

C major scale

Other chord types can evoke different emotions, such as a mysterious or suspenseful atmosphere. Understanding these different chord qualities will greatly assist you in composing chord progressions, as you will know how to create the desired sound and construct the appropriate chords to achieve that particular feeling. Now, let's explore chord qualities.

Chord qualities

Prior to delving into the various chord types, it is crucial to grasp the distinguishing factors that set one chord category apart from another. Furthermore, it can be helpful to look at our interval qualities chart while making your way though this chapter. Here, we present the distinct chord qualities that makes chords unique.

Tone

The tonality of a chord relates to the emotions and atmosphere it conveys. When examining the two primary chord types, major and minor, significant differences in tonal characteristics arise. Major chords generally evoke a sense of brightness and joy, whereas minor chords tend to evoke feelings of sadness or create an atmosphere of suspense. Some chords, such as power chords, are neither major nor minor. This is because they lack the third interval, which is what determines whether a chord is major or minor.

Intervals

Intervals denote the connections between specific tones in a musical context. Within a given key, certain scale degrees hold prominence and distinction compared to others. Chords are made up of intervals. The combination of intervals between notes determines whether a chord is major or minor.

Consonance and dissonance

Consonance and dissonance are two contrasting qualities in music. Consonance refers to sounds that are harmonious and pleasing to the Western musical ear. On the other hand, dissonance represents a more tense and unresolved quality. In most cases, dissonance is typically resolved by transitioning to a consonant chord, providing a sense of stability and resolution in the music. Chords can be consonant or dissonant. A consonant chord will feature consonant intervals.

Resolution

Resolution represents the contrasting counterpart to dissonance and involves highlighting the pivotal notes within a key, such as the dominant or the tonic. Chord progressions commonly exhibit resolution either at the beginning or the end, where the tension is eased and a sense of harmonic stability is achieved.

Chord names

Chords acquire their names from specific qualities that define their sonic characteristics. Understanding the principles behind chord nomenclature is crucial for effectively reading and communicating music. The main factors that contribute to a chord's name are the root note and its quality.

Chord Notations

Chord notations are universally recognized and serve as a shorthand for musicians to quickly understand and interpret chords. They offer a concise way to represent complex chord qualities and structures.

Abbreviations

For instance, a C major seventh chord can be conveniently abbreviated as Cmaj7, while a C minor seventh chord is denoted as Cm7. In addition to abbreviations for major and minor chords, you may come across augmented chords indicated by "aug" or a plus sign (+), and diminished chords represented with a small circle (°) or "dim."

Chord name	Abbreviation	Quality	Key	Example
C Major Triad	C	Major	C	
C Minor Triad	Cm	Minor	C	
C Augmented Triad	Caug or C+	Augmented	C	
C Diminished Triad	Cdim or C°	Diminished	C	
C Major Seventh	Cmaj7	Major Seventh	C	
C Minor Seventh	Cm7	Minor Seventh	C	
C Dominant Seventh	C7	Dominant	C	
C Diminished Seventh	Cdim7 or C°7	Diminished Seventh	C	
C Suspended Seventh	C7sus4	Suspended	C	
C Suspended Second	Csus2	Suspended 2nd	C	
C Suspended Fourth	Csus4	Suspended 4th	C	

Chord types

There are numerous types of chords to play on both guitar and piano, each with different shapes and variations, adding depth and variety to your music. Understanding these chords will expand your musical vocabulary and enhance your playing. Let's delve into the various chord types that can be played on the guitar.

Open chords

Open chords are chords that include one or more strings that are played without being fretted, allowing the string to ring open. These chords are typically played in the first few frets of the guitar and are known for their rich, full sound. They are often the first chords beginners learn due to their simplicity and frequent use in many songs.

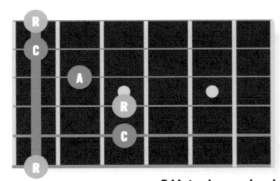

Open C chord

Barre chords

Barre chords use the index finger to press down multiple strings across a single fret, creating a movable "bar" that allows you to play the same chord shape in different positions. This technique makes them versatile and essential for playing a wide range of songs and keys, providing a fuller sound commonly used in various music genres.

F Major barre chord

Power chords

Power chords use two or three notes, typically the root and the fifth, and sometimes the octave. They are easy to play and are movable shapes, making them versatile for different positions on the fretboard. Power chords produce a strong, clean sound, often used in rock, punk, and metal music.

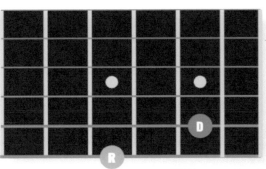

G5 Power chord

Chord types

For practical purposes, we will be focusing on three types of chords. It's essential to recognize three distinct chord types which are triads, seventh chords, and extended chords. These chords which serve practical purposes in music, will equip you with endless possibilities when writing a song or producing a track.

Triad chord

Triads are three-note chords with various qualities: major, minor, diminished, augmented, or suspended. Changing one note can shift the quality, offering expressive options.

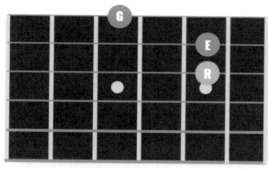

C major triad

Seventh chord

Seventh chords, comprising four notes, include the seventh degree from the scale above the root note. This seventh note is typically a major or minor seventh interval. The major 7th, minor 7th, and dominant 7th are common seventh chords.

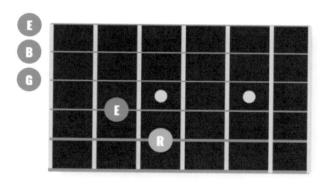

C major seventh chord

Extended chords

Extended chords expand on triads and seventh chords by adding extra notes from their scales: the ninth, eleventh, or thirteenth. These notes are beyond the first octave and correspond to the second, fourth, or sixth scale degrees, such as D representing both the 2nd and 9th notes in the key of C. This enhances harmonic possibilities in music.

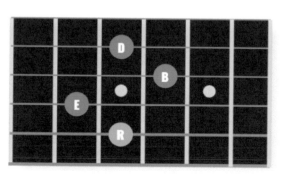

C major nine chord

How chords are built

A chord is built by first selecting the root note, also called the tonic, which is the foundational note and the 1st note in any scale. This root note serves as the base of the chord structure. Next, we select two or more additional intervals from the scale, such as the 3rd and 5th, and build them on the root note to create a chord.

The graph below shows the chromatic scale with its notes represented as numbers in sequence. Think of it as a guitar string, with 0 being the open string and each subsequent number representing a fret on that string.

Since we cannot play chords on a single string, we need to find the same intervals between the different strings on your guitar to form chords. Recognizing these intervals between strings makes it easy to construct chords on your guitar.

For example, in a C major chord, we use the 1st (C), 3rd (E), and 5th (G) notes of the scale to form the chord (1, 3, 5).

The root note (abbreviated as R) is always the reference point in a chord. For example, Gmaj, Gm, and G7 all have the root note G; Emaj, Em, and E7 all have the root note E; and C#maj, C#m, and C#7 all have the root note C#. Different combinations of intervals above the root create various chord types. Now, let's dive deeper into the mechanics behind the different types of chords you'll encounter.

Building chords using formulas

As we know, chords are built from scales. However, on guitar, chords are typically formed using shapes that can be moved up and down the fretboard, allowing them to be played in any key. Despite this practical approach, understanding the theoretical construction of chords is still valuable.

Let's start with the C major chord. This chord includes the root (1), the major third (3), and the perfect fifth (5). Together, these intervals form a basic major triad.

Playing the scale first

By playing the major scale in the key of C, we can easily identify the notes needed to create a major triad, seventh, or extended chord. Because the C major scale can be played in various positions and ways on the guitar, each chord can also be played in multiple positions. To simplify, let's begin with the C major open chord.

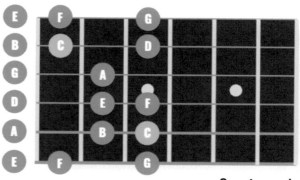

C major scale

The lowest note

The root note doesn't have to be the lowest sounding note in the chord, providing flexibility in chord voicings. This allows for multiple options to start a chord, as long as the 1-3-5 triad structure is maintained across any set of strings.

Doubling notes

On the guitar, we can also include more of the same notes. For example, in the C major chord, you'll notice there are two C's and two E's. Adding more notes that belong to the chord's formula will make the chord sound fuller.

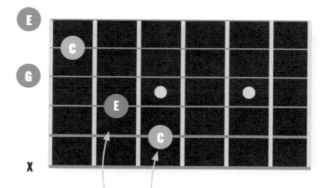

Open C major chord

* Both the E and C notes are featured twice in the C major open chord.

Open chords

Open chords form the foundation of guitar playing. Every beginner guitarist should start by learning open chords. But what exactly are open chords? As the name suggests, open chords utilize the open strings of the guitar, meaning you don't need to press down on every single string. To fret a string means to hold it down at a specific fret, which can be challenging for beginners.

Open chords provide an easier way to play a wide variety of songs on your guitar without needing to fret each string, making them ideal for those just starting out.

With open chords, some of the strings can resonate without being fretted, creating rich and full-sounding chords. The term "open chords" distinguishes them from barre chords. Typically, open chords are played within the first three or four frets of the guitar. Let's get familiar with the essential major open chords every guitarist should know.

Open D chord
Let's start with the D open chord. The D string is 'open,' indicated by the circle at the start of the string. Place your index finger on the second fret of the G string, middle finger on the second fret of the high E string, and ring finger on the third fret of the B string.

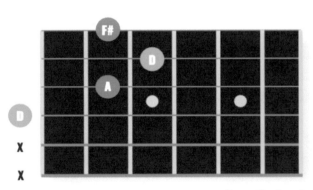

Open D chord

Open A chord
Here's an open A chord. It features two 'open' strings: the A string and the high E string. The other strings are pressed down to form the chord, typically with the index, middle, and ring fingers on the second fret of the D, G, and B strings.

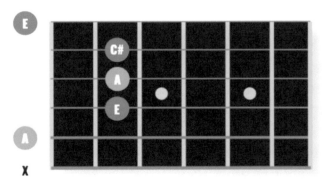

Open A chord

Major open chords

There are 24 commonly used open chords, but it's best to start with the major open chords. These foundational chords are the building blocks of many songs and provide a solid base for your guitar playing.

Open C chord

Now let's explore the open C chord. The G string is 'open,' indicated by the circle at the start of the string. Place your index finger on the first fret of the B string, your middle finger on the second fret of the D string, and your ring finger on the third fret of the A string.

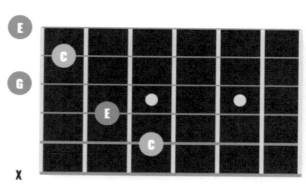

Open C chord

Open G chord

Up next is the open G chord. The D, G, B, are 'open,' indicated by the circles at the start of the strings. Place your middle finger on the third fret of the low E string, your index finger on the second fret of the A string, and your ring finger on the third fret of the high E string.

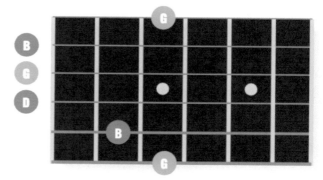

Open G chord

Open E chord

Last but not least we have the open E chord. The low E, B, and high E strings are 'open,' indicated by the circles at the start of the strings. Place your index finger on the first fret of the G string, your middle finger on the second fret of the A string, and your ring finger on the second fret of the D string.

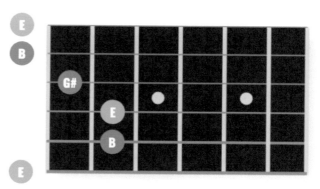

Open E chord

93

Minor open chords

While major chords sound bright and happy, minor chords have a more ominous and sad tone. Interestingly, the only difference between major and minor chords is just one note. As we will demonstrate below, changing one note in a major chord transforms it into a minor chord, resulting in a significant difference in sound. This single note is what makes a chord major or minor, and it's essential to understand which note that is.

In music theory, this note is known as the "3rd." However, what's more important is that you learn to hear the difference between major and minor chords. Recognizing this distinctive sound will deepen your musical understanding and improve your playing.

Open D minor chord

To play an open D minor chord, lower the major third interval, on the high E string from the second fret to the first fret. This change transforms the chord from D major to D minor, giving it a distinct, melancholic sound. This shift changes the chord from bright and consonant to somber and dissonant.

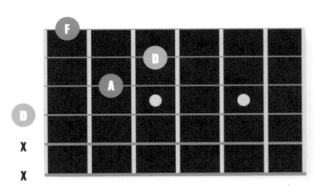

Open D minor chord

Open A minor chord

To play an open A minor chord, lower the major third interval on the B string from the second fret to the first fret. This change transforms the chord from A major to A minor, giving it a distinct, melancholic sound. This shift changes the chord from bright and consonant to somber and dissonant.

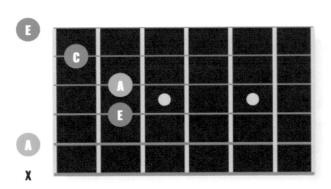

Open A minor chord

Minor open chords

On the guitar, certain notes in open chords are played on open strings, which cannot be easily altered without changing the fingering for the entire chord. Additionally, lowering a note might create awkward stretches or require impossible finger placements. This is why it is often easier and more practical to use barre chords, especially for chords like C minor.

Barre C minor chord

By using a barre chord, you still play the notes C, Eb, and G, which are consistent with the C minor scale formula, ensuring the chord retains its minor quality. The barre chord simplifies finger positioning while maintaining the correct intervals, making it a practical choice for playing minor chords on the guitar.

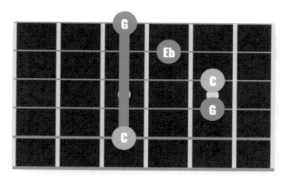

Open C minor chord

G minor chord

To change a G major open chord to a G minor chord, you need to lower the major third interval to a minor third interval. However, since the standard G minor chord cannot be played comfortably in an open position due to the need to lower the B note, the practical way to play a G minor chord is by using a barre chord.

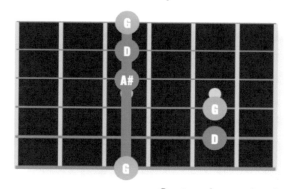

G minor barre chord

Open E minor chord

Changing an E major chord to an E minor chord is a straightforward process because both chords are played in the open position and involve only a single finger movement. To change this to an E minor chord, you need to lower the major third interval (G#) to a minor third interval (G). This can be done by simply lifting our index finger off the G string, leaving it open.

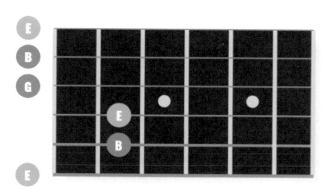

Open E minor chord

95

Barre chords explained

Barre chords can be particularly challenging for beginners due to the finger strength required to press down multiple strings across the fretboard. A barre chord involves using the index finger to press down five or six strings at the same fret, effectively creating a new nut. This technique allows you to move chord shapes up and down the neck.

For instance, a barre chord can be based on an open chord, such as the E major chord. By barring across the first fret and playing the E major shape with all the notes shifted up one fret, you create an F major barre chord. Let's demonstrate this.

E Major chord shape

Let's first examine the E major shape. On your right, you can see the E major chord shape in the open position, which is played at the first fret. In this chord, all the strings are played. Upon closer analysis, you'll notice that this chord resembles a barre chord because the guitar's nut functions as a finger.

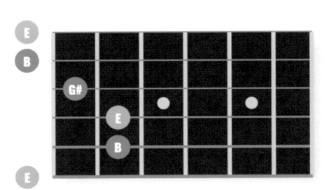

Open E chord

Barring across the first fret

If you move the entire E major shape up one fret and use your index finger to hold down all the strings at the first fret, you create an F major barre chord. This technique effectively shifts the E major chord up by one fret, transforming it into an F major chord.

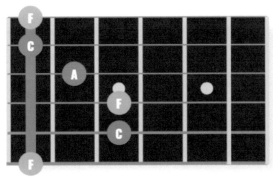

F Major barre chord

It becomes an F chord because the root note is F, located on the first fret of the sixth string (low E string). If you move this entire shape up the neck, the root note changes accordingly, altering the entire chord. Any barre chord that uses this shape will always be a major chord. But more on this later.

Power chords explained

A power chord is a chord that utilizes two or three notes from the scale. The term "power" refers to the powerful and direct sound these chords produce. They are commonly used in metal and rock music, but you can play them on any guitar and in any musical style. However, they might not sound as resonant on an acoustic or classical guitar.

Power chords typically consist of two different notes, but guitarists often play them on three strings. They play the root note, the fifth, and the root note again an octave higher. The root note determines the name of the power chord.

How to play power chords

To create a power chord, you need to play the root note, the fifth, and the root note one octave higher. For example, let's use the C note. The resulting power chord would consist of C (root), G (fifth), and C again (one octave higher).

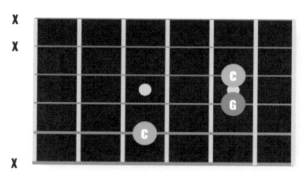

C5 Power Chord

Power chord quality

Power chords are neither major nor minor because they lack the minor or major third interval. The interval between the notes is crucial in power chords, and the repetition of the root note enhances their powerful sound while simplifying the harmony.

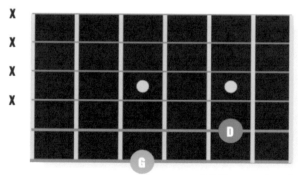

G5 Power chord

Suspended chords

Have you ever seen a chord with "sus" in its name, like Csus2 or Csus4? When played, a sus chord can create a sense of brightness or tension in the music. "Sus" stands for "suspended," as it involves replacing certain notes in the chord with others. Essentially, a sus chord is a major chord with specific notes left out and replaced, transforming it into something new. Let's revisit how a major chord is constructed to understand this better.

A major chord is constructed by combining the first (root), third (3rd), and fifth (5th) notes of a major scale. For instance, a C major chord consists of the notes C, E, and G.

In a suspended chord, the third note is always omitted. The number following "sus" indicates the note that replaces the third. For example, in Csus2, the third is replaced by the second note (D), and in Csus4, the third is replaced by the fourth note (F). Below, you'll see some examples of suspended chords in D open position.

Sus 2
A sus2, or suspended 2nd chord, replaces the third note of the chord with the second note. For example, Csus2 consists of C, D, and G.

Sus4
A sus4, or suspended 4th chord, replaces the third note of the chord with the fourth note. For example, Csus4 consists of C, F, and G.

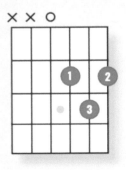

D major

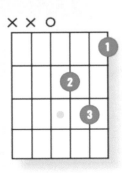

Dm

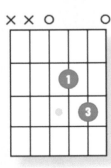

Dsus2

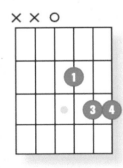

Dsus4

Augmented chords

The augmented (aug) chord and the diminished (dim) chord are two types of triads that are less common in music compared to major and minor chords. The augmented chord is often denoted by a plus (+) symbol, such as C+. When these chords appear in songs, they are usually used sparingly, often as transitional chords between two major chords, adding subtle interest to the harmony.

An augmented chord consists of a root, a major third, and an augmented fifth. "To augment" means to raise, which is precisely what happens with the fifth in an augmented chord. For example, to transform a C major chord into a C+ chord, the notes C, E, and G become C, E, and G#.

Like other chords, augmented chord shapes are movable, but to play them in different keys, you will need to use a barre technique. This allows you to shift the shape up and down the neck while maintaining the correct intervals between the notes.

The diagrams below illustrate some open-position augmented chords. Try playing them on your guitar and notice how their sound differs from major and minor triads.

To augment a seventh chord, you still have to raise the fifth note of the chord by a half step. This changes the chord from a dominant seventh chord (or any other type of seventh chord) to an augmented seventh chord.

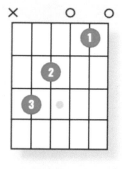

C major

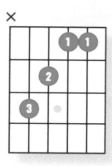

C+

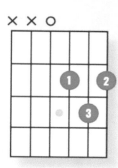

D major

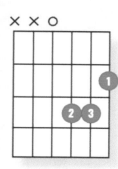

D+

Diminished chords

Diminished chords are triads consisting of a root, a minor third, and a flattened fifth (also known as a diminished fifth). The first two notes are identical to those in a minor triad; the difference lies in the fifth. In a minor chord, the fifth is a perfect fifth above the root. In a diminished chord, the fifth is lowered by a half step, creating a tritone above the root note.

While augmented chords raise the fifth, diminished chords lower it. Diminished seventh chords are created by adding a seventh to a diminished triad. Typically, the seventh appears in an upper voice, though it can be positioned anywhere in the chord structure. However, it is rare for the seventh to be the lowest pitch in a diminished seventh chord.

Half-Diminished Chords (Minor Seventh Flat Five Chords)

Commonly used in jazz and classical music, these chords include a root, a minor third, a diminished fifth, and a minor seventh. For example, a C minor seventh flat five (Cm7b5) chord consists of C (root), Eb (minor third), Gb (diminished fifth), and Bb (flat seventh). It resembles a C minor seventh chord but with the fifth lowered by a half step. These chords are popular in jazz and progressive rock.

Fully Diminished Seventh Chords (Diminished Seventh Chords)

These chords contain a root, a minor third, a diminished fifth, and a diminished seventh (double flat seventh). To form a diminished seventh chord, lower the minor seventh by a half step. For instance, lowering the Bb in a Cm7b5 chord by a half step to Bbb (which is enharmonic to A natural) transforms it into a Cdim7 chord.

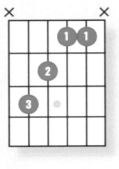

C+   Cdim

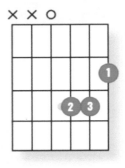

D+

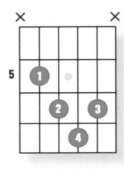

Ddim

Dominant chords

Dominant chords are similar to major chords but include a flattened seventh. The term "dominant" or "Dom" is rarely included in the chord name. Therefore, when you see chords labeled as C7, E7, F#7, etc., These are all dominant chords and should not be confused with major or minor chords. For example, C7, Cmaj7, and Cm7 are all different chords. Additionally, chords like C7, C9, C11, and C13 are all variations of dominant chords.

A C major scale contains seven notes: C, D, E, F, G, A, and B. The dominant chord from this scale has a root of G, a third of B (the seventh note of the C major scale), and a fifth of D (the ninth note, assuming the scale extends into the next octave).

How to form a dominant chord

To form a dominant seventh chord, an additional note is added to the triad. This note is a minor seventh above the root. In our example of a dominant chord built from the C major scale, the seventh note would be F. Therefore, a G dominant seventh chord (G7) consists of the notes G, B, D, and F.

Dominant chords are used in various musical contexts to create tension, facilitate modulation, enrich harmonic progressions, and provide a sense of closure or transition. Their strong pull towards resolution makes them an essential element in both classical and contemporary music.

Below, you will see examples of dominant chords and how they differ from major triads, using both the C major and D major scales.

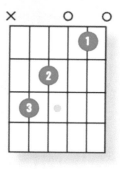

C major

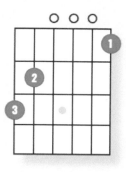

G7

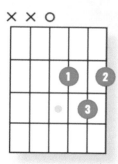

D major

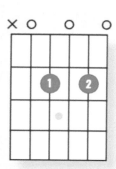

A7

The chromatic scale

As mentioned earlier, a chord is a musical structure built from two or more notes. For example, the C major chord consists of the notes C, E, and G. These notes are the building blocks of the C major chord. However, when learning chord construction, it's far more effective to think of these building blocks as intervals rather than individual notes.

By understanding chords in terms of intervals, you only need to learn each chord shape once. You can then move the shape up or down the fretboard to play higher or lower versions of the same chord. This approach simplifies learning and will become clearer as we progress.

Just like scales, chords are constructed from a series of intervals. As previously mentioned, having a basic understanding of intervals is essential before constructing chords. To recap, there are 12 intervals in total, which comprise what is known as the chromatic scale.

Semitones	Interval name	Abbreviation	Notes in Key of C	Characteristic
0	Unison	P1	C - C	Open consonance
1	Minor 2nd	m2	C - Db	Sharp dissonance
2	Major 2nd	M2	C - D	Mild dissonance
3	Minor 3rd	m3	C - Eb	Soft consonance
4	Major 3rd	M3	C - E	Soft consonance
5	Perfect 4th	P4	C - F	Mild consonance
6	Tritone	A4/d5	C - Gb	Ambiguous
7	Perfect 5th	P5	C - G	Open consonance
8	Minor 6th	m6	C - Ab	Soft consonance
9	Major 6th	M6	C - A	Soft consonance
10	Minor 7th	m7	C - Bb	Mild dissonance
11	Major 7th	M7	C - B	Sharp dissonance
12	Octave	P8	C - C	Open consonance

All chord formulas

Understanding chord formulas and scales simplifies the process of creating chords. By mastering major and minor scales in various keys and learning chord formulas, you can independently construct chords and apply them to any key. Below, we provide all the chord formulas, illustrated using piano diagrams for clarity. The same principles apply to the guitar.

Chord name	Formula	Quality	Example
C Major	1-3-5	Major	
C Major 6	1-3-5-6	Major	
C Major 7	1-3-5-7	Major	
C Major 9	1-3-5-7-9	Major	
C Major 11	1-3-5-7-9-11	Major	
C Major 13	1-3-5-7-9-11-13	Major	
C Sus 2	1-2-5	Sus	
C Sus 4	1-4-5	Sus	
C Dominant 7	1-3-5-b7	Dominant	
C Dominant 9	1-3-5-b7-9	Dominant	
C Dominant 11	1-3-5-b7-9-11	Dominant	
C Dominant 13	1-3-5-b7-9-11-13	Dominant	
C Minor	1-b3-5	Minor	
C Minor 6	1-b3-5-6	Minor	
C Minor 7	1-b3-5-b7	Minor	
C Minor 9	1-b3-5-b7-9	Minor	
C Minor 11	1-b3-5-b7-9-11	Minor	
C Diminished	1-b3-b5	Diminished	
C Diminished 7	1-b3-b5-b7	Diminished	
C Augmented	1-3-#5	Augmented	

Chord inversions

Chords on the piano are often played in a structured manner, with the lowest note as the root, followed by the third, and then the fifth, creating a neat and tidy arrangement. However, this order is not mandatory. In fact, guitarists rarely play chords in this strict sequence because it can be difficult to grip them that way.

On the guitar, the physical layout of the fretboard and the way chords are fingered often necessitate a different approach. Guitarists frequently use chord inversions, which involve rearranging the order of notes so that the third or fifth might be the lowest note instead of the root.

C major first inversion
The first inversion of a chord involves making the third the lowest note (the bass) of the chord. In the C major chord, the third is the E note. Therefore, the first inversion of a C major chord has E as the bass note. The most common notation used to represent chord inversions is a slash.

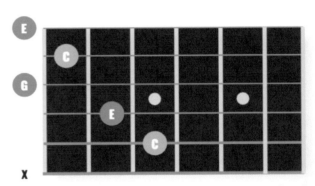

C major open chord

Include the E string
To play the first inversion of a C major chord in the open position, include the low E string while playing the open C major chord. This makes the E note the lowest note.

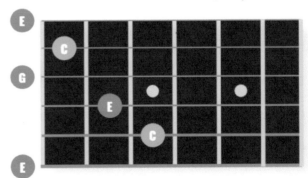

C Major first inversion or C/E

Barre chord shape
You can also play the first inversion by using a barre chord shape. Barre the D, G, and B strings at the 5th fret and play the 7th fret on the A string (E note). This places E in the bass position.

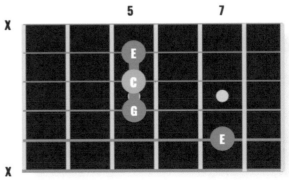

C Major first inversion barre chord or C/E

Second inversion

A chord can be inverted multiple times based on the number of notes it contains. For a triad, which consists of three notes (root, third, and fifth), there are two possible inversions: first inversion, with the third as the lowest note, and second inversion, with the fifth as the lowest note.

A seventh chord, which includes four notes (root, third, fifth, and seventh), can be inverted three times: first inversion with the third in the bass, second inversion with the fifth in the bass, and third inversion with the seventh in the bass.

How many times you can invert
Generally, the number of possible inversions for any chord is one less than the number of notes in the chord. Understanding and using these inversions allows for smoother voice leading and greater harmonic variety in music.

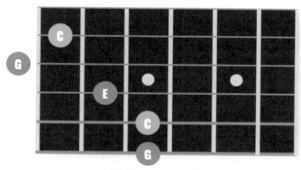

C Major second inversion or C/G

C major Second inversion
In the second inversion of a chord, the lowest note is the fifth. In the C major chord, the fifth is the G note. Therefore, the second inversion of the C major chord is notated as C/G, indicating that G is the bass note.

Barre chord shape
You can also play the second inversion of a C major chord using a barre chord shape. To do this, barre across the third fret and press down on the fifth fret of the D, G, and B strings.

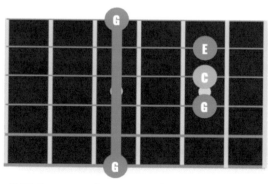

C Major second inversion barre chord or C/G

Third inversion

In the third inversion, the lowest note is the seventh degree of the chord. Special attention is required when the seventh is a major seventh (7M), as it is a semitone below the root (1st degree). This close interval can create a sense of tension or discomfort, often referred to as "chromaticism," because the tonic is just a half-step above the bass note.

This can give the impression of "missing" the bass by playing the tonic slightly higher than expected. However, when the seventh is minor, this issue is not present. Here is an example of the 3rd inversion for the Cmaj7 and C7 chords, where the major 7th is the B note and the minor 7th is the Bb note.

C major seventh third inversion

In the third inversion of a chord, the lowest note is the seventh. In the C major seventh chord (Cmaj7), the seventh is the B note. Therefore, the third inversion of the Cmaj7 chord is notated as Cmaj7/B, indicating that B is the bass note.

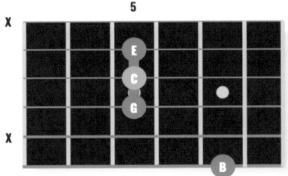

C Major 7th third inversion

C minor seventh third inversion

With a C minor seventh chord (Cm7) in the third inversion, you only need to move two notes. By simply lowering the E to Eb, and B to Bb, you change the chord from Cmaj7 to Cm7 while keeping the Bb in the bass, thus creating a C minor seventh chord in the third inversion (Cm7/Bb).

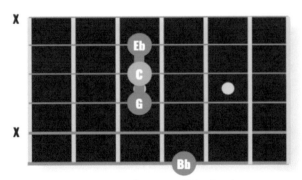

C minor 7th third inversion

Explore chord inversions

There are countless shapes for forming inverted chords on the guitar. Here, we present just a few to introduce the concept. Explore and discover other shapes for these chords and seek out inversions for additional chords as well.

Major inversions (C-F)

Chord inversions might be easier to understand when visualized on a piano keyboard. Therefore, we have included a chart of inversions for major and minor chords on the piano. Remember, chord inversions are simply different arrangements of the notes within a chord. The same principles apply to the guitar.

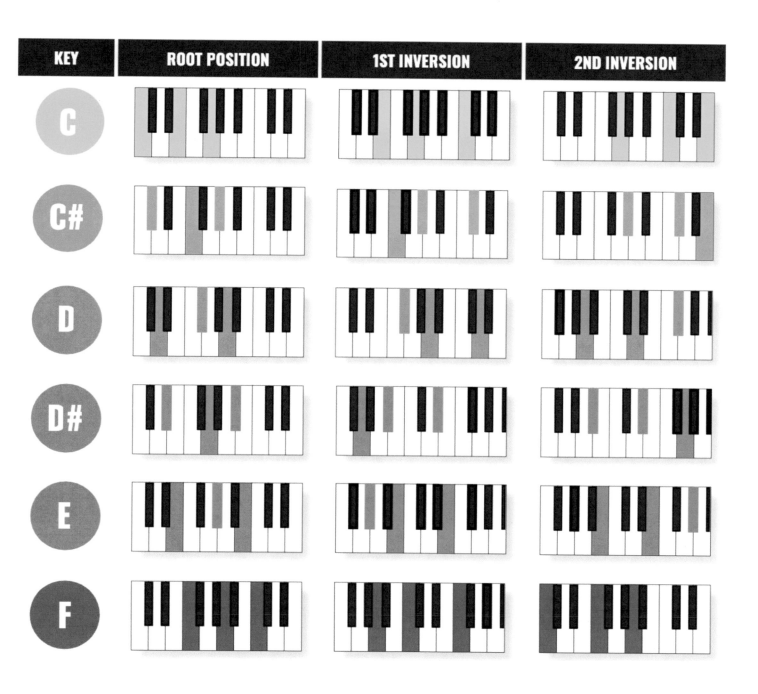

KEY	ROOT POSITION	1ST INVERSION	2ND INVERSION
C			
C#			
D			
D#			
E			
F			

Major inversions (F-B)

Chord inversions might be easier to understand when visualized on a piano keyboard. There-fore, we have included a chart of inversions for major and minor chords on the piano. Remember, chord inversions are simply different arrangements of the notes within a chord. The same principles apply to the guitar.

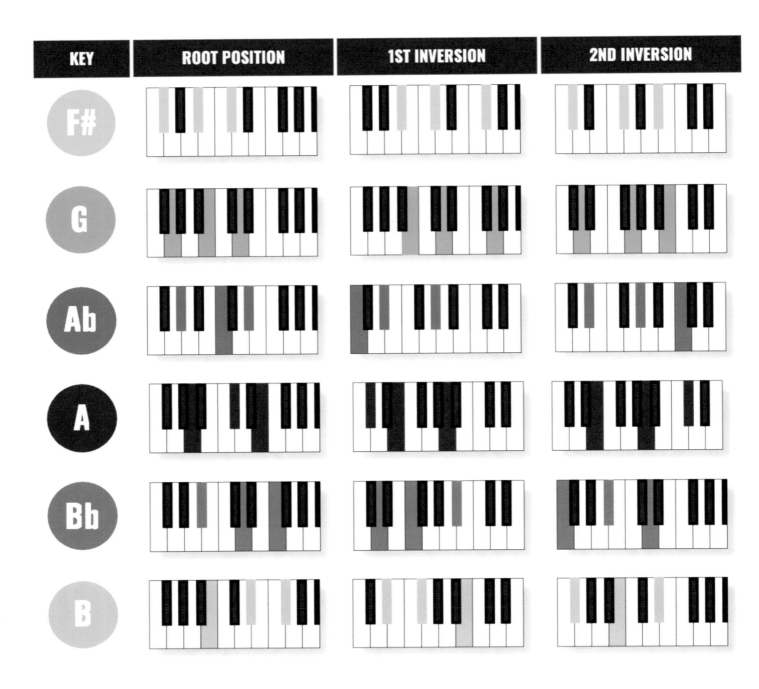

KEY	ROOT POSITION	1ST INVERSION	2ND INVERSION
F#			
G			
Ab			
A			
Bb			
B			

Minor inversions (C-F)

Chord inversions might be easier to understand when visualized on a piano keyboard. Therefore, we have included a chart of inversions for major and minor chords on the piano. Remember, chord inversions are simply different arrangements of the notes within a chord. The same principles apply to the guitar.

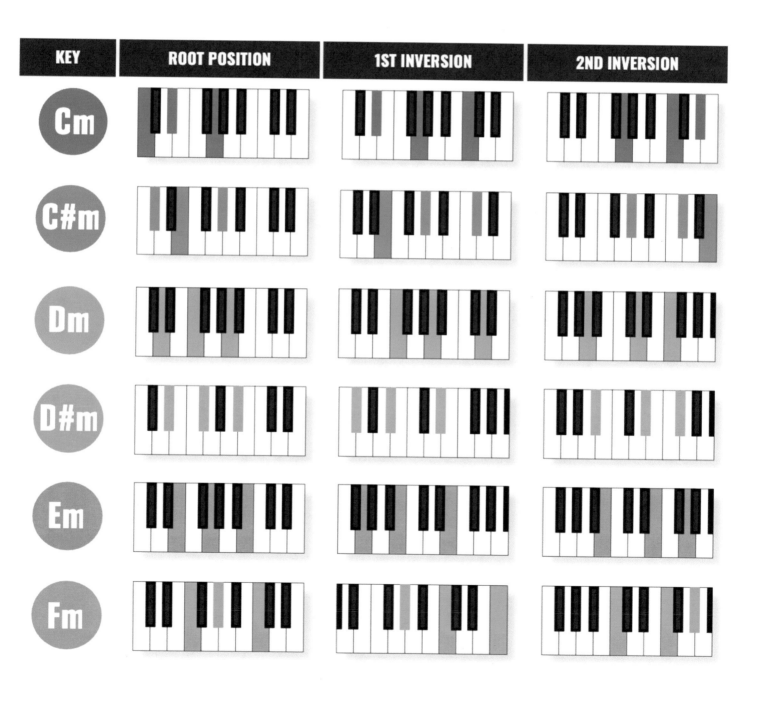

Minor inversions (F-B)

Chord inversions might be easier to understand when visualized on a piano keyboard. Therefore, we have included a chart of inversions for major and minor chords on the piano. Remember, chord inversions are simply different arrangements of the notes within a chord. The same principles apply to the guitar.

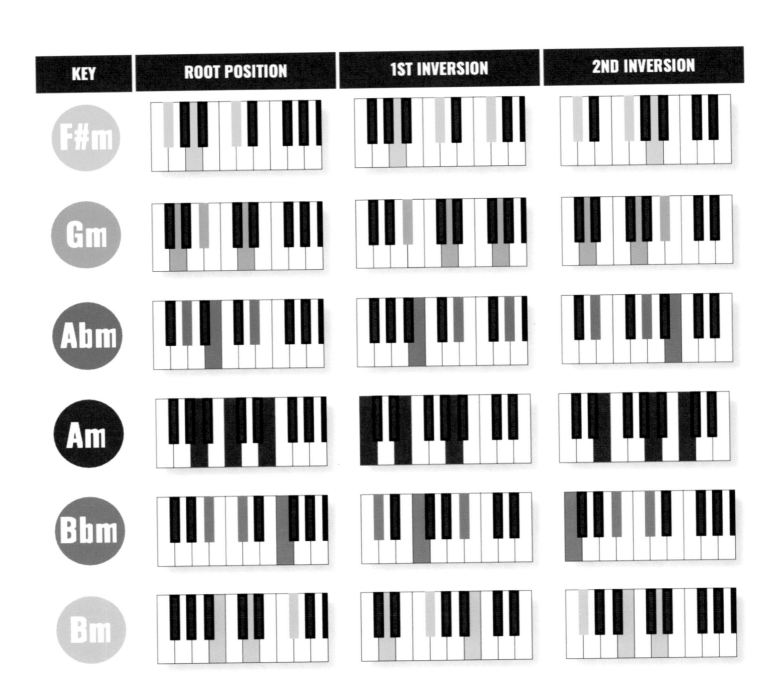

| KEY | ROOT POSITION | 1ST INVERSION | 2ND INVERSION |

Key takeaways

In this chapter, we explored the concept of melodic and harmonic intervals, the construction of chords using chord formulas, different chord types, and the art of chord inversion to lend them a distinct character and facilitate smoother playability. Take your time to diligently practice these newfound concepts and integrate them into your ongoing music projects. The more you incorporate these techniques, the more they will seamlessly become a part of your musical repertoire.

Melodic interval

In music, a melodic interval is the pitch difference between two consecutive notes in a melody, determining whether one note is higher or lower than the other. It's described by terms like "major third" or "perfect fourth," indicating the specific distance and quality of the interval. Understanding melodic intervals is crucial for shaping a melody's mood and expression.

Harmonic interval

A harmonic interval in music occurs when two different notes are played or sung simultaneously. These intervals, described as "major thirds," "perfect fifths," and so on, contribute to chords and harmony in music, shaping its overall texture and emotional impact.

Chords

Chords in music are harmonious combinations of three or more notes, formed by specific formulas from major and minor scales. Extensions involve adding extra notes for complexity (e.g., seventh or ninth chords), while inversion rearranges notes within the chord for unique voicings and smoother transitions. Understanding these concepts is vital for creating expressive music.

Chord qualities

Chords in music are harmonious combinations of three or more notes, formed by specific formulas like major or minor chords. Extensions involve adding extra notes for complexity (e.g., Seventh or ninth chords), while inversion rearranges notes within the chord for unique voicings and smoother transitions. Understanding these concepts is vital for creating expressive music.

Chords to practice

This guitar chords chart includes essential Major, Minor, 7, Minor 7, 6, m6, Sus 4, and Diminished chords, perfect for expanding your chord knowledge and enhancing your playing.

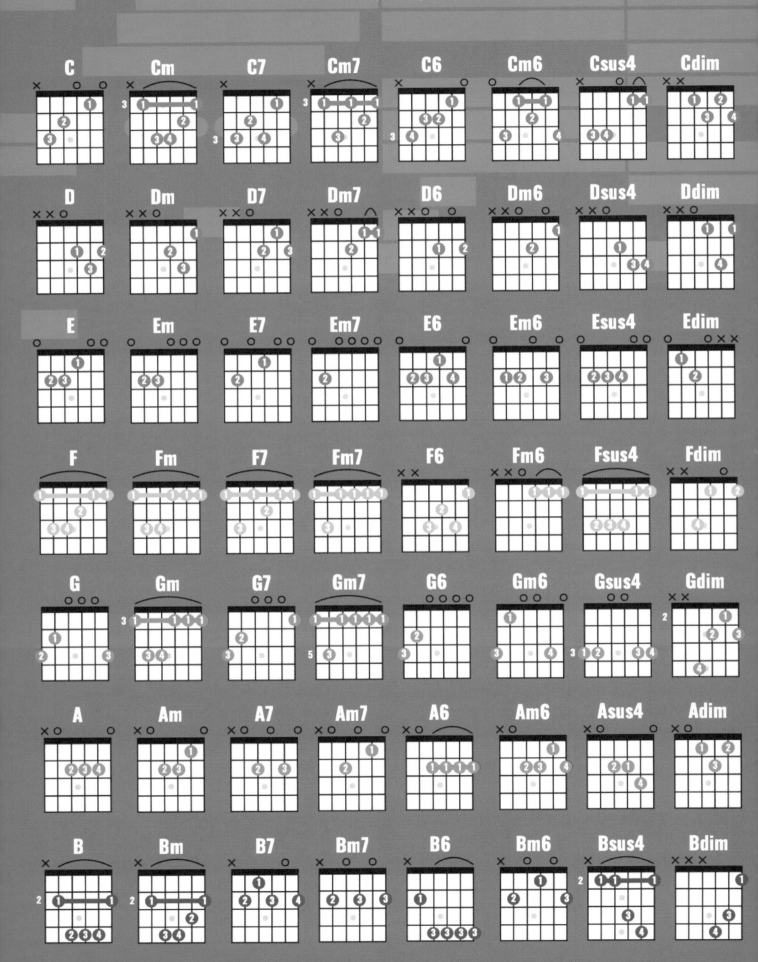

Jargon guide

Music theory can be a complex subject, and even more so with its specialized vocabulary. This guide is here to assist you in comprehending and defining the terms you've come across in this chapter or to refresh your memory.

Consonance

Consonance in music is the pleasing combination of elements like chords or intervals, evoking stability and emotional impact, contrasting with dissonance's tension and instability. It's crucial for creating pleasing melodies and harmonies.

Unison

Unison in music refers to two or more musical parts or voices playing or singing the same note at the same pitch, creating a single unified sound. It produces a harmonically stable and consonant effect, enhancing the strength and clarity of the musical passage.

Dissonance

Dissonance in music is the tension caused by unstable chord or interval combinations, contrasting with consonance's stability. It adds emotional depth, often resolving into harmonious sounds, enhancing musical expressiveness.

Perfect interval

A perfect interval in music refers to a specific type of interval between two notes with a harmonically stable and consonant sound. These intervals include the perfect unison (P1), perfect fourth (P4), perfect fifth (P5), and the perfect octave (P8).

Voicing

Chord voicings in music refer to how the notes of a chord are arranged among instruments or voices, impacting the chord's sound and texture.

Tonic

The tonic is the first note of a scale, serving as the home or central pitch in a key, providing a sense of resolution and stability in a musical piece.

Chord qualities

Chord qualities in music refer to the distinct characteristics and emotional qualities of different chord types. These qualities include major chords, which sound bright and happy; minor chords, which evoke a somber or sad feeling; diminished chords, known for their tense and unstable sound; and augmented chords, which create a sense of tension and unpredictability.

5. CAGED SYSTEM
UNLOCKING THE FRETBOARD

By now, you should have a solid understanding of how scales form the foundation of music, serving as the building blocks for melody, harmony, and improvisation. You've also learned how chords are derived from these scales, providing the harmonic backbone that supports and enriches musical compositions.

As you continue your journey in guitar theory, it's time to delve into one of the most powerful tools for mastering the fretboard: the CAGED system. This system is an essential framework that connects the scales and chords you've learned, enabling you to navigate the entire fretboard with ease and confidence.

‹ WHAT YOU WILL LEARN

- The CAGED system
- How to move shapes
- Connecting the shapes
- Unlocking the fretboard

‹ WHAT DO YOU NEED

- Any six string guitar
- Whiteboard markers
- A smartphone

‹ SKIP THIS LESSON IF

- You know the CAGED system

What is the CAGED system?

The CAGED system utilizes common open chord shapes to divide the guitar neck into five distinct sections. This approach simplifies the fretboard by demonstrating the relationship between these open chord shapes and the arrangement of notes and intervals on the guitar. Once you understand this relationship, the fretboard is no longer a confusing grid of notes. Instead, it becomes a series of interconnected shapes and patterns.

The CAGED guitar theory system is based on five fundamental open chord shapes: C, A, G, E, and D, hence the name CAGED. Each of these chord forms is movable, allowing them to be played in various positions along the fretboard. Typically, this is achieved by barring the notes that fall on the same fret, enabling the chords to maintain their shape while being transposed to different keys.

First, let's examine each chord shape in its open form. After that, we'll explore how to move these shapes up and down the fretboard.

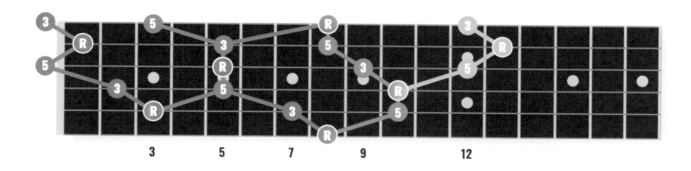

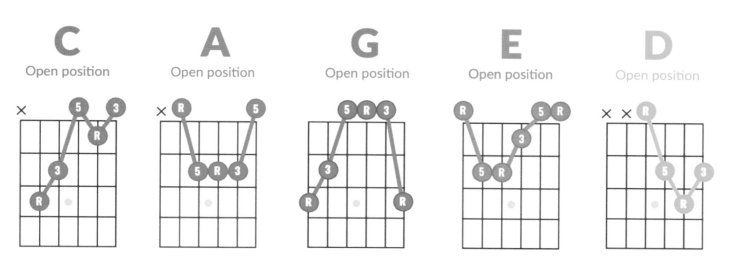

Moving chord shapes (C-A)

The entire CAGED system is built around these five shapes, as they can be moved up and down the neck. Using these open chords, you can play any chord with any of the five shapes. For example, if you want to play a D chord, you can move the C shape up two frets. However, keep in mind that the open strings are no longer in tune when the shape is moved.

To correct this, you need to place a barre two frets up, where the open strings would be. Similar to moving a C major chord up a whole step on a piano to form a D major chord, this approach works on the guitar as well. Let's explore how we can form other chords using the C shape.

Open C chord

If you move the open C chord up two frets, it becomes a C-form D chord. Since the C shape is no longer in an open position, you'll need to barre across strings 1, 2, and 3. Notice how the scale degrees remain the same.

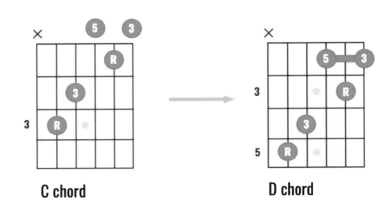

C chord

D chord

Open A chord

Similarly, when you move the open A chord shape up to the 2nd fret, it becomes a B chord in the A form. Since this shape is no longer in the open position, you'll need to barre across the strings at the 2nd fret.

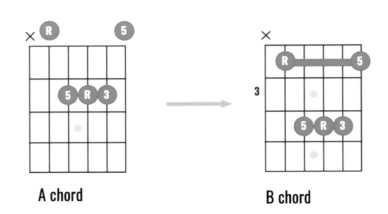

A chord

B chord

116

Moving chord shapes (G-E)

Just as you can shift chord positions up and down the piano to create chords in different keys, the CAGED system allows us to move chord shapes along the guitar fretboard. By using any of the open chord shapes and applying a barre across the strings, you can easily play any chord in any key. The key is to remember that when you move a chord shape up the fretboard, the root note of the chord changes, altering the chord's name.

For instance, when you move an E major shape up by one fret, and use a barre to cover the open strings, you create the next chord which is an F major chord. Similarly, moving a C major shape up one fret gives you a C# major chord. The process works by shifting the entire shape, with the barre effectively acting as the new "nut" of the guitar.

Now, let's explore how this works in practice by moving the G and E open chord shapes up the fretboard to create Ab and F chords, respectively. By placing the G shape at the third fret with the appropriate barre across the first fret, you'll form a Bb major chord. Likewise, shifting the E shape up one fret and barring at the second fret transforms it into an F major chord.

Open G chord

If you move the open G chord up one fret, it becomes a G-form Ab (G#) chord. Since the G shape is no longer in an open position, you'll need to barre across the strings at the first fret.

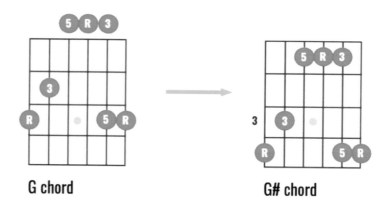

G chord   G# chord

Open E chord

Similarly, when you move the open E chord shape up one fret, it becomes an F chord. Since the E shape is no longer in an open position, you'll need to barre across strings all strings on the first fret.

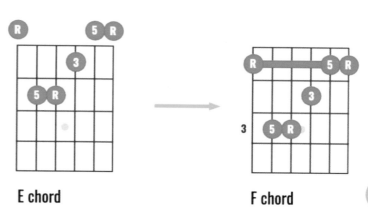

E chord   F chord

Moving chord shapes (D)

Now imagine the guitar fretboard as a piano keyboard. When you play any of the open chords from the CAGED system, you can move them up or down the fretboard to create the next chord in the musical alphabet.

Considering the musical alphabet, which includes flats and sharps (C, C#, D, D#, E, F, F#, G, G#, A, A#, B, C), you'll see that if you move your C open chord shape up one fret, you get a C# chord. Move it up another fret, and you get a D chord. Moving it up again gives you a D# chord, and so on.

Now let's explore the last open chord shape from the CAGED system: the D chord. We'll transform this D chord into an F chord. According to the musical alphabet, which can be visualized linearly on a piano keyboard, moving up three semitones (half steps) from D brings us to F. Similarly, if we move our open D chord up three frets on the guitar, we will create an F chord.

Open D chord

By moving the open D chord shape up three frets, we create an F chord in the D form. Since we only play the highest four strings, there's no need to barre across the third fret.

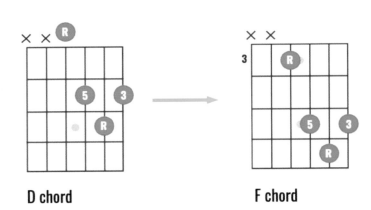

D chord   F chord

Understanding the arrangement of notes in the musical alphabet allows you to transpose any CAGED chord shape into any key. Imagine the guitar fretboard as a piano keyboard, where each fret represents a key on the piano.

By sliding the chord shapes up and down the neck, you unlock the fretboard, providing countless possibilities to play chords anywhere along it. This technique significantly expands your ability to play in different keys and positions.

CAGED is a pattern

The true power of the CAGED system is realized when you apply the concept of movable chord shapes to a single chord. This system logically maps out the fretboard, allowing any given chord to be played all over the neck using the CAGED chord forms. Each chord shape seamlessly connects to the next in a predictable CAGED pattern, providing a comprehensive framework for navigating the fretboard.

For example, if we play each CAGED chord shape with the root note as C, you can play a C chord in various positions along the fretboard. When you do this, you'll notice how each chord shape connects to the next, creating a continuous pattern.

Memorizing the root note

To effectively use the CAGED system, you must memorize where the root note is in each chord shape. This root note, often the lowest note in terms of pitch, is crucial for identifying and moving the chord shape. In the CAGED system, the lowest root note is typically found on the low E, A, or D string.

Developing movable chord shapes

Once you understand where the root note is and can identify each open chord shape without using the open strings, you can start playing these shapes anywhere on the neck. This practice transforms open chord shapes into movable chord shapes.

Applying the CAGED system with C as the root

Let's play each CAGED shape with the root note as C. When you do this, you will get the following chords, as shown in the graphic below. Notice how the root of each chord is C.

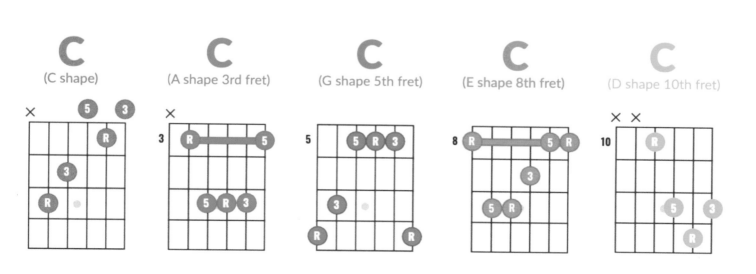

C (C shape) C (A shape 3rd fret) C (G shape 5th fret) C (E shape 8th fret) C (D shape 10th fret)

Connecting the shapes

By playing each CAGED shape with C as the root, you begin to see how these shapes interlock and connect across the entire fretboard. Each shape shares one or more notes with the next, creating a seamless transition from one chord shape to another. This interconnectedness covers the entire neck, allowing you to play chords in any position and move fluidly along the fretboard.

Now, take a look at the illustration below. Notice how all the CAGED chord shapes are intricately linked together across the fretboard? This connectivity is the key to unlocking the full potential of your guitar playing. By understanding how these shapes interrelate, you can transition smoothly between chords and scales, enabling you to play in any key with confidence. This not only enhances your rhythm playing but also significantly boosts your improvisational skills.

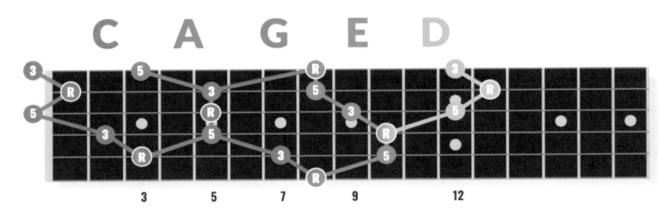

At first glance, the CAGED system might seem elementary—just moving familiar chord shapes around the neck. However, the true power of this system becomes apparent when you delve deeper into its application, particularly in relation to scales. By mastering the CAGED shapes and learning how to connect them across the fretboard in various keys, you establish a strong foundation for understanding and navigating scales.

This framework is invaluable for improvisation. With the CAGED system, you can confidently navigate the fretboard without getting lost, using these shapes as reference points to construct melodies, solos, and lead guitar parts. It provides a road-map that makes the entire fretboard accessible, ensuring you're always aware of where you are, no matter the key or position.

In essence, the CAGED system is more than just a collection of chord shapes; it's a comprehensive tool that bridges the gap between chords and scales, offering you the ability to play with freedom and creativity across the entire guitar neck.

Connecting the shapes

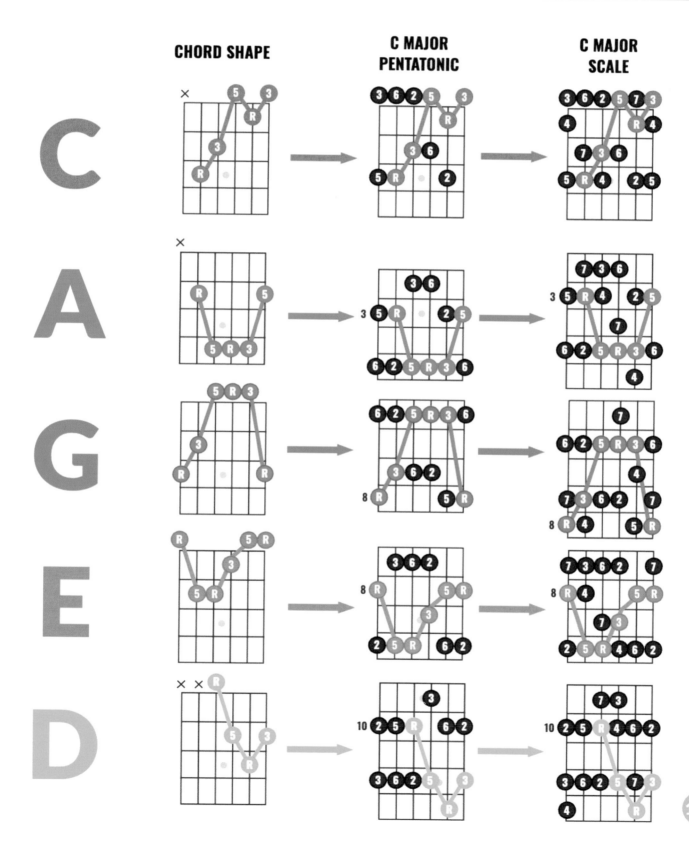

CHORD SHAPE   **C MAJOR PENTATONIC**   **C MAJOR SCALE**

C

A

G

E

D

Connecting the shapes

The CAGED system is not only essential for mastering chord shapes across the fretboard; it also plays a crucial role in learning and applying scales in various positions. Here's how the CAGED system enhances your understanding of scales

Learn the Patterns

By learning the scale patterns associated with each CAGED chord shape, you can seamlessly transition from one scale pattern to the next, just as you do with chord shapes. This interconnectedness allows you to explore the entire fretboard, moving both horizontally (up and down the neck) and vertically (across the strings) with confidence.

Visualize the Intervals

The CAGED system also helps you visualize the intervals within a scale relative to the chord shapes. For example, by knowing the root note within the C shape, you can easily identify key intervals like the third, fifth, and octave in that position. This understanding is crucial for improvisation and melody creation, enabling you to craft musical ideas with precision and creativity.

The illustration on the right demonstrates this concept. Notice how each CAGED shape forms the foundation of its corresponding scale, and how these shapes interconnect to create a continuous, navigable pattern across the fretboard.

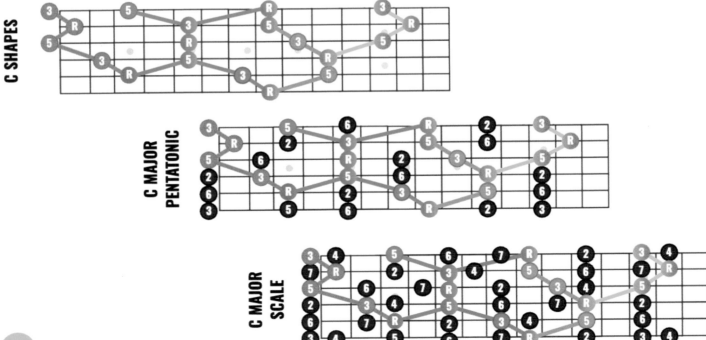

Key takeaways

In this lesson, we explored the importance of the CAGED system in unlocking the fretboard and connecting chord shapes across the guitar. By understanding how each CAGED shape corresponds to specific chord forms and scale patterns, we delved into how these shapes interconnect to create a comprehensive map of the fretboard.

As we progress further into guitar theory, the complexity can increase. If you ever feel overwhelmed, it's essential to pause, review each lesson carefully, and ensure a solid understanding before moving on to the next topic. Taking this approach will help you master the CAGED system effectively and avoid confusion.

The CAGED system

Just as knowing the layout of a city helps you navigate it more efficiently, the CAGED system provides a road-map for the guitar fretboard. It breaks down the neck into five familiar chord shapes (C, A, G, E, D), allowing you to play chords and scales in any key, anywhere on the fretboard. Understanding the CAGED system gives you the tools to move fluidly across the guitar, enabling better improvisation and chord transitions.

Connecting chord shapes

The CAGED system is like a puzzle where each piece connects seamlessly with the next. By learning how these chord shapes interlock, you can navigate the fretboard with confidence, transitioning smoothly from one chord position to another. This interconnectedness not only aids in playing chords but also in finding scale patterns that fit perfectly within these shapes.

Visualizing scales

Visualizing scales through the CAGED system is like seeing the fretboard in high definition. Each chord shape corresponds to a specific scale pattern, allowing you to play major and minor scales, as well as modes, all over the neck. This understanding helps you to craft melodies, solos, and harmonies that are perfectly in tune with the key of the song.

Jargon guide

Music theory can be a complex subject, and even more so with its specialized vocabulary. This guide is here to assist you in comprehending and defining the terms you've come across in this chapter or to refresh your memory.

The CAGED system

CAGED System: A method for visualizing and playing chord shapes across the guitar fretboard, based on the open chord shapes C, A, G, E, and D.

Open chord shapes

Chord shapes that include open strings, typically played in the first few frets of the guitar.

Movable shapes

Chord or scale shapes that can be shifted up and down the fretboard without changing their structure, allowing you to play the same chord or scale in different keys.

Barring notes

Pressing down multiple strings across a single fret with one finger, typically the index finger, to form chords or play multiple notes simultaneously.

Guitar's nut

The small piece of material at the top of the fretboard that guides the strings and defines the starting point of the scale length, just before the headstock.

Root note

The fundamental note of a chord or scale, which determines its key and name. For example, the root note of a C major chord is C.

Arpeggios

The notes of a chord played individually rather than simultaneously, often practiced within the CAGED shapes to develop fretboard fluency.

Pentatonic scales

Five-note scales that fit within the CAGED shapes, commonly used in improvisation and soloing.

6. PROGRESSIONS & ROMAN NUMERALS

Now that you have a solid understanding of keys, scales, intervals, chords, and the CAGED system, it's time to elevate our knowledge further. In this chapter, we delve into the world of chord progressions and Roman numerals.

The ability to craft your own original chord progressions from the ground up is a skill that can significantly enhance your music and take your abilities to the next level.

This chapter is more extensive than previous ones, so take your time going through it and don't hesitate to use the QR codes when needed.

‹ WHAT YOU WILL LEARN

- Chord progressions
- Diatonic chords
- Roman numerals
- Scale degrees

‹ WHAT DO YOU NEED

- Any six string guitar
- MIDI Keyboard
- Piano
- A smartphone

‹ SKIP THIS LESSON IF

- You can create progressions from scratch
- You know the diatonic chords
- You know what roman numerals stand for

What are chord progressions?

Chord progressions are a series of chords played in a specific sequence within a scale, establishing a tonality based on a key. You can have multiple chord progressions within a song varying from verse to chorus etc. Creating melodies and harmonies both rely on staying within the key signature or related keys for harmony. To make your music captivating, establish connections between chords for smooth harmonic transitions.

Chords in a progression harmonize when they're in the same key. In a key (or scale), specific chords naturally fit each note, known as diatonic chords. Let's explore how chords are built from the C Major scale notes.

Presented below are the foundational seven chords that can be fashioned utilizing the notes encompassed within this scale. When talking about chord progressions, we refer to these notes as 'scale degrees'.

C	D	E	F	G	A	B
E	F	G	A	B	C	D
G	A	B	C	D	E	F
C major	D minor	E minor	F major	G major	A minor	B diminished

Clearly evident is the structured sequence that chords within a scale adhere to. This sequence unfolds as major, minor, minor, major, major, minor, and diminished. Remarkably, this chord pattern remains consistent across all twelve major keys, showcasing the unchanging nature of chords fashioned from the scale's notes.

Diatonic chords explained

We just demonstrated the concept of diatonic chords built from the C major scale on the piano, as it might be easier to grasp visually. However, the same principle applies to the guitar. Within the C major scale, you can play seven diatonic chords on the guitar.

These are chords that are derived from the notes of a specific scale. In the C major scale (C, D, E, F, G, A, B), you can build seven diatonic chords, one for each note of the scale.

The visualization below shows how these chords are formed and played on the guitar fretboard, making it easier to understand and apply the theory in practice. By learning these diatonic chords, you can enhance your understanding of harmony and improve your ability to play in different keys.

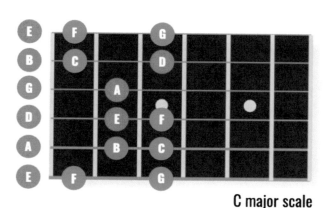

C major scale

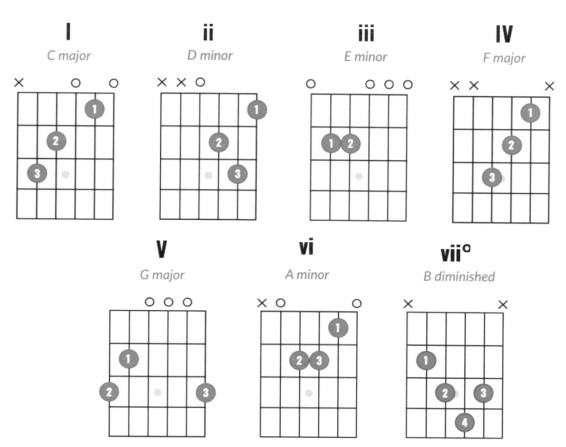

How to find chords in a key

In any musical scale, there are seven chords known as diatonic chords, each assigned a specific number using Roman numerals in music theory. Let's take the key of C as an example, which comprises the notes C-D-E-F-G-A-B. To find the diatonic chords in this key, you simply play a triad from each of these notes and moving up the scale till you reach the B note. The pattern then repeats itself, creating those same seven chords an octave higher.

In the key of C major, the diatonic chords can be easily identified by following a simple pattern.

Start with a major triad chord based on the note C. Then, move the entire chord shape up, one note at a time, until you reach B.

By doing this, you will discover the seven diatonic chords that naturally fit within the key of C major.

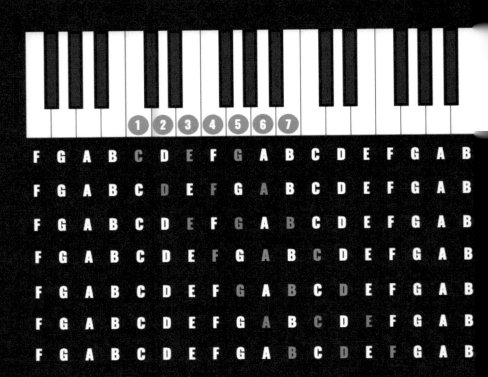

Each chord is assigned a number from 1 to 7. Referencing the chart, you'll observe the chords formed at various positions within the scale. Commencing with the C note, the initial chord is a C major triad. Progressing, you encounter a D minor chord, followed by an E minor, an F major, a G major, an A minor, and finally, the seventh position gives rise to a B diminished chord. This set of chords will remain the same in any other major key.

You have the flexibility to perform a 1-4-5 chord progression not only in C major but also in various other major keys. This chord sequence maintains its consistent sound across these keys, while the distinctive tonal quality shifts based on the specific key you're using.

Roman numerals

Since a number doesn't tell you that much in itself, opting for Roman numerals instead of chord names enables you to effortlessly compose chord progressions in any desired key. Roman numerals tell you more than just its position, also its quality.

In music capital letters stand for major chords, small letters for minor chords, and a small circle is added for diminished chords. This way, we simplify how we show different types of chords in written music. This is what it looks like in C major:

I-ii-iii-IV-V-vi-vii°

I	ii	iii	IV	V	vi	vii°
Major	Minor	Minor	Major	Major	Minor	Diminished
C	Dm	Em	F	G	Am	B°
Db	Ebm	Fm	Gb	Ab	Bbm	C°
D	Em	F#m	G	A	Bm	C#°
Eb	Fm	Gm	Ab	Bb	Cm	D°
E	F#m	G#m	A	B	C#m	D#°
F	Gm	Am	Bb	C	Dm	E°
Gb	Abm	Bbm	Cb	Dd	Ebm	F°
G	Am	Bm	C	D	Em	F#°
Ab	Bbm	Cm	Db	Eb	Fm	G°
A	Bm	C#m	D	E	F#m	G#°
Bb	Cm	Dm	Eb	F	Gm	A°
B	C#m	D#m	E	F#	G#m	A#°

Minor key chords

So the Roman numerals are used to substitute the numeric position of a note within a scale. They symbolize the chord that can be constructed from the respective note. Moving forward, it's important to commit these numerals to memory. As you contemplate scales, endeavor to associate the notes not merely by their names or numbers, but by their corresponding Roman numerals. This practice will greatly enhance your understanding of the chords that can be formed from each note.

To forge chords within natural minor keys, we must follow an alternative arrangement. The initial, fourth, and fifth notes yield minor chords, the third, sixth, and seventh generate major chords, and the second note transforms into a diminished chord. This leaves us with:

i-ii°-III-iv-v-VI-VII

Now, take a moment to observe the arrangement provided and establish connections with the notes derived from the A natural minor scale. By doing so, you'll gain a precise understanding of which note corresponds to each chord. Keep in mind that this sequence of chords remains consistent across all minor keys, unaffected by the specific scale you choose to play.

This allows us to create the following chords:

A	B	C	D	E	F	G
C	D	E	F	G	A	B
E	F	G	A	B	C	D
A minor	B diminished	C major	D minor	E minor	F major	G major

Diatonic minor key chords

We previously illustrated the concept of diatonic chords using the A minor scale on the piano, which might be easier to visualize. However, the same concept applies to the guitar. In the A minor scale, you can play seven diatonic chords on the guitar.

These chords are built from the notes of the A minor scale (A, B, C, D, E, F, G), with one chord corresponding to each note.

The diagrams below shows how these chords are formed and played on the guitar fretboard, aiding in the comprehension and practical application of this theory. By learning these diatonic chords, you will deepen your understanding of harmony and enhance your ability to play in various keys.

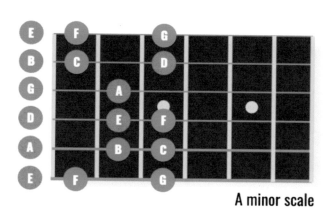

A minor scale

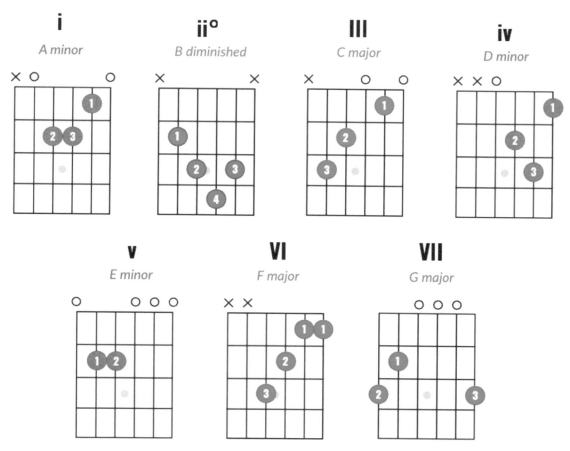

All minor chords

By this point, you should have a solid grasp of crafting chords from any note within major or minor scales. Moving forward, we'll teach you how to use this information to build your own chord progressions, utilizing the roman numerals. This approach provides a structured way to sequence chords, guiding the harmonic journey of your music.

However, before we proceed, let's begin with an overview of the array of chords you can generate within any minor scale. Dedicate time to practicing these chords for each minor key and strive to commit them to memory. Equally beneficial is doing the same for the chords in major keys.

i	ii°	III	iv	v	VI	VII
Minor	Diminished	Major	Minor	Minor	Major	Major
Am	B°	C	Dm	Em	F	G
Bbm	C°	Db	Ebm	Fm	Gb	Ab
Bm	C#°	D	Em	F#m	G	A
Cm	D°	Eb	Fm	Gm	Ab	Bb
C#m	D#°	E	F#m	G#m	A	B
Dm	E°	F	Gm	Am	Bb	C
Ebm	F°	Gb	Abm	Bbm	Cb	Db
Em	F#°	G	Am	Bm	C	D
Fm	G°	Ab	Bbm	Cm	Db	Eb
F#m	G#°	A	Bm	C#m	D	E
Gm	A°	Bb	Cm	Dm	Eb	F
G#m	A#°	B	C#m	D#m	E	F#

Scale degrees explained

You might wonder: "How do I choose chords to follow in a key?" In music, a scale consists of ascending or descending notes, with each note labeled as a "degree" based on its position in the scale. These degrees are assigned numerical values.

Understanding these scale degrees is crucial for crafting chords, creating chord progressions, and analyzing melodies and harmonies. Each degree in a key has a specific role in guiding chord and melody progression, influencing the direction and quality of the music. This knowledge empowers composers and musicians to create engaging and harmonically satisfying chord patterns. Below you'll see what scale degrees look like.

Degree	Function	Example note (C Major)	Roman numeral
1	Tonic	C	I
2	Supertonic	D	ii
3	Mediant	E	iii
4	Subdominant	F	IV
5	Dominant	G	V
6	Submediant	A	vi
7	Leading tone	B	vii°
8 or 1	Tonic	C	I

The tonic, subdominant, and dominant scale degrees are considered the most crucial ones due to their pivotal roles in establishing the tonal center, creating harmonic tension, and shaping the overall progression of a musical piece.

These scale degrees form the foundation of many chord progressions and help define the tonality and structure of the music. The tonic provides stability, the subdominant introduces anticipation, and the dominant introduces tension, making them essential elements in shaping the emotional and harmonic landscape of a composition.

Scale degrees functions

Let's take a moment to break down what each note in a scale does. This way, when you're coming up with chord progressions, you'll have a clearer picture of how each note can add something special. On the right side, we have visualized what chord each scale degree would create in the key of C Major. It's like having a toolkit to make your music sound just the way you want it to!

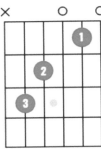

The tonic (I) / C Major

Let's start with the tonic. At a scale's core is the cornerstone: the 1st degree, termed the tonic. As the "keynote," it shapes identity and indicates the musical key. Positioned first in a diatonic scale, it lends its name to the scale.

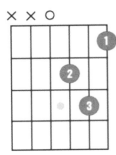

The supertonic (ii) / D minor

The supertonic, which is the second note in a scale, helps melodies move smoothly and can make the music feel a bit exciting. It sometimes goes to the first note of the scale or other important notes to make the music more interesting and give it a sense of where it's going.

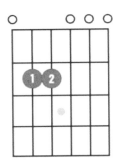

The mediant (iii) / E minor

The mediant, which is the third note in a scale, often resolves to the tonic, which is the first note of the scale. This resolution creates a sense of closure and stability in the music. In a minor key, the resolution from the mediant chord (III) to the tonic chord (i) can also provide a similar feeling of resolution and rest.

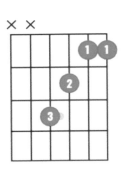

The subdominant (IV) / F Major

The subdominant, the fourth note in a scale, adds anticipation and sets up change in music. It usually goes to the dominant chord, the fifth note. This creates tension because the dominant chord wants to resolve to the tonic chord, the first note.

Scale degrees functions

The dominant (V) / G Major

The fifth note in a scale, called the dominant, creates tension and anticipation in music. It strongly resolves to the first note, known as the tonic, offering a satisfying sense of completion and stability. This interplay shapes many chord progressions and the overall harmony of a piece.

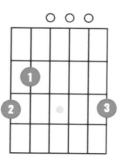

The submediant (vi) / A minor

The sixth note in a scale, called the submediant, adds contrast and variety to music. It often resolves to the first note, the tonic, creating a sense of completeness and stability. The submediant can change a chord progression's mood or direction, with its resolution to the tonic providing a satisfying conclusion.

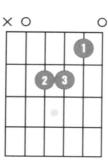

The leading tone (vii°) / B diminished

The seventh note in a scale, called the leading tone, creates tension and strongly pulls towards the first note, the tonic, like a musical cliffhanger. This desire for resolution contributes to the feeling of closure and adds excitement and anticipation to music.

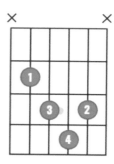

In short

It's beneficial to familiarize yourself with the distinct functions and roles of each scale degree within a musical scale. This understanding acts as a guiding compass when crafting chord progressions, enhancing your ability to compose harmonically engaging and emotionally resonant music.

135

Major vs minor functions

Now, let's explore the functions of scale degrees in minor keys, noting the differences from major keys.

- **Tonic (1st degree):** In both major and minor keys, the tonic remains a point of resolution and stability.

- **Dominant (5th degree):** Similar to major keys, the dominant in a minor key strongly desires to resolve to the tonic, creating a sense of resolution and closure.

- **Subdominant (4th degree):** The subdominant in a minor key can still lead to the dominant as in a major key, but its role might feel slightly different due to the differences in emotional quality between major and minor tonalities.

- **Mediant (3rd degree):** In a minor key, the mediant's role is different from its major key counterpart. The mediant chord often plays a supporting role and doesn't necessarily have the same level of resolution tendencies.

- **Submediant (6th degree):** In a minor key, the submediant can have a unique harmonic role and might not necessarily resolve in the same way as in a major key.

- **Leading Tone (7th degree):** The leading tone in a minor key typically still has a strong tendency to resolve to the tonic, creating a sense of resolution and finality.

While there are similarities in the way scale degrees resolve in major and minor keys, the emotional qualities and tonal characteristics of minor keys can lead to some differences in how these resolutions are perceived and utilized in chord progressions.

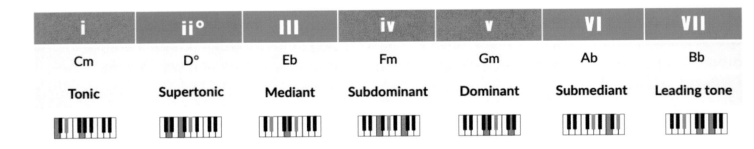

i	ii°	III	iv	v	VI	VII
Cm	D°	Eb	Fm	Gm	Ab	Bb
Tonic	Supertonic	Mediant	Subdominant	Dominant	Submediant	Leading tone

Major chord motions

You're likely aware that you can leverage the functions of scale degrees to guide the direction of your chord progression. This understanding provides valuable insights as you embark on creating chord sequences. Yet, there exist established formulas that can further simplify the process, making it even more straightforward to discover chord progressions that harmonize effectively.

Initially, you'll need to select the key in which you wish to perform. Is it major or minor? Afterward, it's the selection of the second chord following your I chord that establishes the foundation for your chord progression. The main rule is, if it sounds good, it is good. While there aren't strict guidelines dictating the subsequent chord after your I chord, certain harmonic choices have proven to be consistently effective.

Chord progression guide
Below, we've visualized the direction your chords like to follow in major keys. This is more of a tool than a strict rule to follow. By exploring the pathways outlined in this tool, you'll discover chord progressions that resonate beautifully and flow naturally. Remember, a chord can be used more than once in a progression. Use your ears and listen to what works well and what does not.

Chord	Best followed by	Function	Example
I (C major)	Any chord	Tonic	
ii (D minor)	V, VI, IV, VII	Supertonic	
iii (E minor)	VI	Mediant	
IV (F major)	ii, vii, V	Subdominant	
V (G major)	ii, VII, I, vi	Dominant	
vi (A minor)	IV, ii, I	Submediant	
vii° (B diminished)	V, I	Leading tone	

Minor chord motions

While there are some similarities between the motions of chords in major and minor keys, there are a few notable differences due to the distinct emotional qualities of these tonalities.

Both major and minor keys utilize the tonic chord (I or i) as a point of rest and resolution. The subdominant chord (IV or iv) and the dominant chord (V or v) play roles in building tension and leading towards resolution in both major and minor keys.

Differences

In major keys, the overall feel tends to be more uplifting and joyful. Chords often progress in a way that reinforces this sense of positivity. In minor keys, the emotional character is often more introspective or melancholic.

Chords can have more varied motions that convey a range of feelings, including vulnerability, yearning, or darkness. The submediant (vi) chord in a minor key, for example, takes on a unique emotional weight that differs from its major key counterpart. Similarly, the vii° chord (leading tone) in a minor key has a more pronounced sense of tension.

In essence, while there are parallels in chord motions, the nuanced emotional qualities of major and minor keys result in distinct patterns of chord progression that evoke contrasting feelings and atmospheres. You'll find a chord motions formula for minor keys below.

Chord	Best followed by	Function	Example
i (C minor)	Any chord	Tonic	
ii° (D diminished)	v, VI, iv, VII	Supertonic	
III (Eb major)	i, VI	Mediant	
iv (F minor)	ii°, VII	Subdominant	
v (G minor)	VII, i	Dominant	
VI (Ab major)	iv, ii°	Submediant	
VII (Bb major)	i, III	Leading tone	

What about other chords?

If you're new to crafting chord progressions from the ground up, beginning with basic triads can be a valuable starting point. This approach allows you to establish a chord progression that holds a pleasant quality. As you become more comfortable, you can introduce a wide array of embellishments into your triad-based progressions, exploring numerous creative pathways.

Suspended chords

When creating chord progressions, you can include other chords such as the suspended 2nd, 4th. Have a look at the table below to see how you can replace a major or minor chord with a suspended chord. Sus chords are often used to create tension that can be resolved by returning to the original major or minor chord. For example, you might use a Gsus4 (G-C-D) before resolving it to a G major (G-B-D) in a progression.

Extended chords

Having delved into chord extensions during the previous lesson, now's the time to apply that learning. Extend your chords by integrating the 7th, 9th, or 11th scale degrees into your triads, instantly elevating their depth and complexity. This simple addition will grant your chords a fuller and more captivating quality.

Inversions

The true beauty of many chords emerges in their first or second inversion. Therefore, investing time in perfecting chord inversions is invaluable. Mastery of inversions not only adds captivating allure to your chord progressions but also facilitates effortless execution.

Degree	Triad chord	Seventh chord	Suspended 2nd	Suspended 4th
I				
ii				
iii				
IV				
V				
vi				
vii°				

The I-IV-V progression

Having familiarized yourself with the mechanics of chord progressions, let's now provide you with a valuable reference point. We'll delve into a collection of well-known chord progressions frequently employed in music.

The 1-4-5 chord progression is one of the most prevalent and recognizable sequences in music. This progression, known for its simplicity and effectiveness, starts with the tonic chord (I) and then smoothly transitions to the subdominant chord (IV), creating a sense of musical movement and anticipation. Finally, it resolves to the dominant chord (V), providing a satisfying conclusion. All three chords are major in this progression, contributing to its characteristic sound and harmonious resolution.

I-IV-V in A Major

A prime and widely recognized illustration of the I-IV-V chord progression can be found in "Stir It Up" by the iconic reggae figure, Bob Marley. This musical piece exclusively employs major chords derived from the A Major scale.

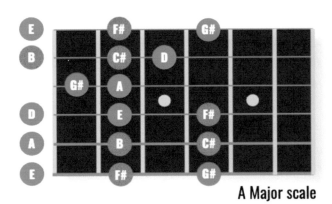

A Major scale

When writing this song, the three major diatonic chords from the scale were used which are the first, fourth and fifth. On the adjacent side, you'll find the scale illustrated with its corresponding notes. Just beneath, you'll discover the chords sourced from each note, collectively shaping the foundation of this composition.

Bob Marley - Stir It Up
Progression - I-IV-V
Key: A Major

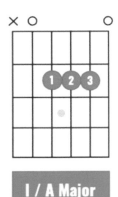

I / A Major

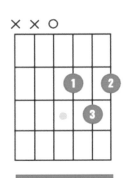

IV / D Major

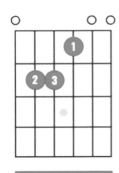

V / E Major

The I-V-vi-IV progression

An enduringly popular chord sequence is the I-V-vi-IV progression, celebrated for its widespread presence in the musical landscape. Across an array of genres, from pop to punk to country, this progression has woven itself into the very fabric of music.

The allure of this sequence is found in the unique emotional depth carried by each successive chord. Once you become attuned to this progression, its ubiquitous presence in the domain of pop music becomes evident, consistently seizing your focus. It finds its place in various iconic tracks, such as Akon's "Don't Matter," U2's "With or Without You," Adele's "Hello," and Eminem and Rihanna's "Love the Way You Lie," to name a few notable examples. Now, let's delve deeper into the intricacies of this chord progression below.

I-V-vi-IV in D Major

In U2's "With Or Without You," the mesmerizing I-V-vi-IV chord progression in the key of D shines. Among the seven diatonic chords in this key, the band deftly opts for three major and one minor chord. This choice profoundly shapes the song's evocative musical ambiance.

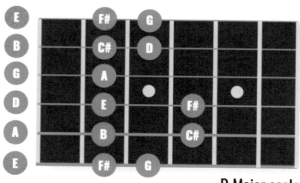

D Major scale

U2 - With Or Without You
Progression - I-V-vi-IV
Key: D Major

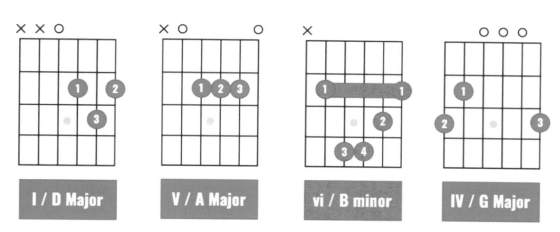

| I / D Major | V / A Major | vi / B minor | IV / G Major |

The IV-I-V-vi progression

The IV-I-V-vi chord progression is highly acknowledged for its delightful and uplifting quality. This sequence of chords finds broad application across diverse musical genres, fostering a feeling of resolution, positivity, and familiarity. Its timeless charm has earned it the monikers of both the "pop-punk progression" and the "four-chord progression."

Clearly evident is the chord progression's unconventional departure from the tonic as it initiates on the fourth chord. Instead of adhering to the anticipated tonic chord as a starting point, the progression intriguingly begins with the fourth chord of the key. This calculated divergence from the norm imparts a sense of unexpectedness. This choice not only captures the listener's attention but also generates a subtle undercurrent of tension by momentarily setting aside the anticipated commencement.

IV-I-V-iv in Db Major

This chord progression is most prominently recognized in Rihanna's hit song "Umbrella". Within this specific musical context, the song is in the key of Db major. The chords are drawn from the fourth, first, fifth, and sixth scale degrees of the key.

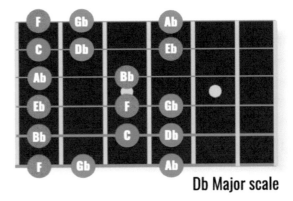

Db Major scale

Rihanna - Umbrella
Progression - IV-I-V-vi
Key: Db Major

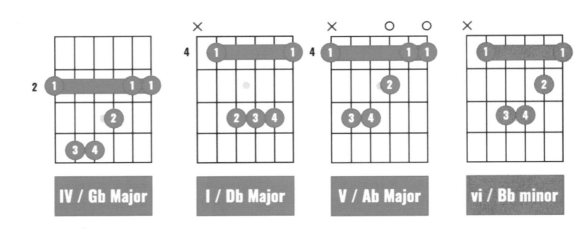

| IV / Gb Major | I / Db Major | V / Ab Major | vi / Bb minor |

Tips for chord progressions

If you've reached this point, give yourself a well-deserved pat on the back. Navigating chord progressions can be quite a challenge. Keep in mind that the ultimate judge of success is the way something sounds. Even though there's a wealth of theory and guidelines surrounding chord progressions, remember that having an innate sense for them, by relying on your musical intuition, can be equally effective. However, understanding the available tools and possibilities remains valuable. Here are a handful of tips to ensure your chord progressions truly shine.

First determine the key

When crafting chord progressions, always begin with the key your musical piece will be in. If you have a melody idea in mind or a sample you'd like to add chords to, try to determine the key it is in. Once the key has been identified, find out what chords you can play within that key. Then, you can experiment with different chords to initiate a chord progression.

Use your ears

The ultimate essence lies in the way something resonates to the ears, a principle that holds true across the realm of music. If the progression from a I chord to a iii chord strikes a pleasing chord, there's every reason to incorporate it. In this realm, it's not about rigid rules, but rather about embracing guiding principles that offer creative direction.

Start small

As you explore chord progressions, begin with simplicity as your foundation. Start by using triads to capture the fundamental essence and overall sonic landscape of your progression. Once you've identified a pleasing framework, enhance it by introducing embellishments that infuse depth and complexity into your chord progression, resulting in a more intricate and compelling musical journey.

Embellishments

To make your chord progressions more exciting, try changing up your chords. Play them in different ways, like flipping them around or using unique versions. You can also use different kinds of chords, like ones that have a suspended feeling. These changes will add a cool twist to your music.

Key takeaways

This chapter's aim was to transform your outlook on chord progressions. As you've seen, it's not as complex as it may seem. Think of a scale as a gift waiting to be unwrapped. Inside, you'll discover diatonic chords that align with that scale, each denoted by Roman numerals. With practice, it all becomes easier. Ensure you master the diatonic chords for both major and minor keys; this alone will unlock limitless possibilities for crafting songs.

Chord progression

A chord progression is a sequence of chords played in succession, forming the harmonic backbone of a piece of music. It defines the order and arrangement of chords, creating the musical structure and mood of a composition.

Diatonic chords

Diatonic chords are chords built using the notes from a particular musical scale without introducing additional notes from outside the scale. They naturally fit within a given key and contribute to the harmonies of a piece.

Roman numerals

Roman numerals are a symbolic notation system used in music theory to represent the position of a chord within a scale or key. They provide a standardized way to label chords and understand their function within a musical context.

Scale degrees

Scale degrees are the specific positions or steps within a musical scale, each with a unique numerical label. They are used to describe the relationship between notes within a scale, helping to identify and understand the intervals and structure of melodies and chords in music.

Jargon guide

Music theory can be a complex subject, and even more so with its specialized vocabulary. This guide is here to assist you in comprehending and defining the terms you've come across in this chapter or to refresh your memory.

Chord functions

Chord functions in music are the roles that chords play within a harmonic progression. These functions include tonic (providing stability), dominant (creating tension), and subdominant (offering a transitional role). Chord functions are essential in shaping the musical structure, tension, and resolution in a composition.

Resolve

Resolve in music refers to the satisfying conclusion of a musical phrase or progression. It typically involves the resolution of dissonant or tense musical elements to harmonious and stable ones, creating a sense of closure and fulfillment in the music.

Extended chords

Extended chords in music are chords that go beyond the basic triad (three-note) or seventh chord (four-note) structure by including additional chord tones, such as the ninth, eleventh, or thirteenth. These chords add complexity and color to harmonies, creating a rich and lush sound in various musical genres.

Sus chords

Suspended chords in music are chords that temporarily replace a traditional major or minor chord. They create a sense of tension and expectation, often resolving to a major or minor chord, adding a unique and expressive quality to the music.

Chord motions

Chord motions in music refer to the movement or changes between chords in a progression. They dictate how chords transition from one to another, influencing the overall harmonic structure and emotional flow of a piece.

Embellishments

Embellishments in music are decorative musical elements, like trills or grace notes, used to enhance a melody or passage, adding ornamentation and expression.

Easy   +/- 15 min   4 sections

7. MUSIC NOTATION
LEARN TO READ MUSIC

Now, let's explore a more traditional music theory topic which is what we call music notation. Notation helps us understand the symbols in music theory and lays the foundation for grasping rhythm and timing, which we'll cover in the next chapter.

In this chapter, we'll start with the basics. If your goal is to read and play music from traditional sheet music, you may need to study this subject more in-depth. However, this chapter will give you a strong foundation in understanding notation.

‹ WHAT YOU WILL LEARN

- Guitar tablature
- Basic musical notation
- Notes and note values
- Reading notes

‹ WHAT DO YOU NEED

- Any six string guitar
- MIDI Keyboard

‹ SKIP THIS CHAPTER IF

- You know guitar tablature
- You know music notation
- You understand notes and note values
- You can already read music

Guide to musical notation

In music theory, notation consists of symbols guiding musicians on how to perform a composition. While we won't delve deeply into traditional music theory, grasping basic note symbols can be helpful. You can explore traditional notation later in your musical journey. For now, let's focus on the basics. There are various forms of musical notation to suit different genres and preferences, including:

Standard Notation on 5-line Staves

A traditional method prevalent in classical music, employing a system of five horizontal lines on which musical notes are placed.

Lead Sheets

Widely embraced in jazz, pop, and rock, these sheets present a melody on a 5-line staff accompanied by chords represented through letter and number symbols.

Guitar Tablature

Particularly favored by rock guitarists, this form illustrates notes and chords directly on the guitar's neck, aiding players in identifying positions.

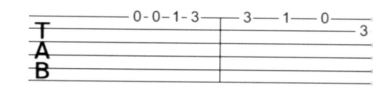

Bar-based MIDI Notation

Primarily existing in digital environments, it relies on MIDI technology and computer screens to depict musical arrangements.

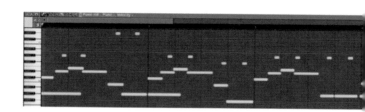

Guitar tablature explained

Guitar tablature, commonly known as "tab," is a simplified form of musical notation that makes it easier for beginner guitarists to pick up songs quickly. While it shares some features with traditional music staff notation—such as indicating which notes to play, and sometimes their duration, and the techniques to use—guitar tabs offer a distinct advantage: they specifically show you where to play the notes on the guitar.

This is especially useful because the guitar allows the same note to be played in multiple locations on the fretboard. Tabs eliminate the guesswork by clearly indicating the exact strings and frets to use, making it easier for beginners to start playing right away. Unlike traditional musical notation, which can be complex and time-consuming to learn, guitar tablature provides a more accessible entry point for those eager to start playing without needing to master standard notation first.

How its written

Tablature is written using six lines, each representing one of the six strings on a guitar. The strings are arranged on the tab in the following order, from top to bottom:

Numbers indicate frets

Numbers are placed on these lines to indicate which fret should be pressed on each string. In this example, you should press the third fret of the A string with your left hand and pluck the string with your right hand.

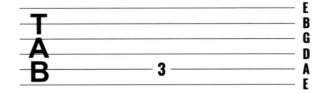

Sequences

When numbers appear in sequence, each note should be played consecutively. In the example on your right, you would start by playing the 5th fret of the D string, followed by the 7th fret of the D string, then move to the 5th fret of the G string, and continue in that order.

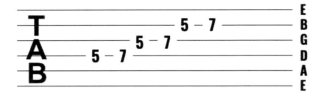

Guitar tab techniques

There are many techniques you can use when playing the guitar, including hammer-ons, pull-offs, bends, and slides. In tablature, these techniques are represented by specific symbols and lines. Here are some key ones you should be familiar with.

Hammer-on

This technique involves striking the string on a specific fret with your left hand alone, without using the right hand to pluck the string. The note is produced solely by the left hand. In tablature, this can be indicated by the letter "h" next to the fret number, or by a line connecting two notes.

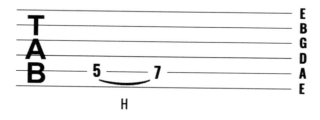

Pull-off

A pull-off involves releasing the finger of your left hand from a pressed string, allowing the note to ring out without the need for the right hand to pluck the string. The notation for a pull-off is similar to that of a hammer-on, as shown in the example on your right. When you combine hammer-ons and pull-offs in a smooth, connected sequence without re-picking the string, it's called legato.

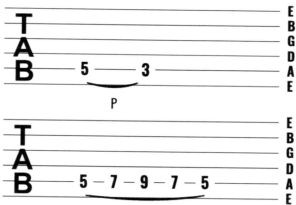

Bends

A note bend involves stretching a string with your left-hand fingers up or down to change the pitch, aiming to achieve the sound of a higher fret without actually moving your finger to that fret. If the bend raises the pitch by one fret, it's called a half bend. When the pitch is raised by two frets, it's known as a whole step bend or full bend. You can bend the string even further to reach higher notes—the more you bend the string, the higher the pitch, allowing you to achieve pitches several frets ahead.

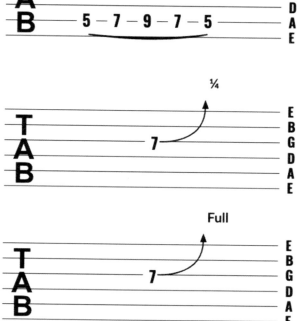

Guitar tab techniques

There are many techniques you can use when playing the guitar, including hammer-ons, pull-offs, bends, and slides. In tablature, these techniques are represented by specific symbols and lines. Here are some key ones you should be familiar with.

Slide

This technique involves sliding your left-hand finger horizontally across the fretboard from one fret to another, gliding smoothly over the frets until you reach the desired note. In tablature, this is represented by a dash.

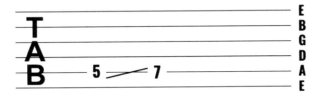

In this example, you should press the 5th fret on the A string and then slide your finger up to the 7th fret, allowing the string to ring out continuously throughout the entire movement. Similarly, a downwards dash stands for sliding downwards.

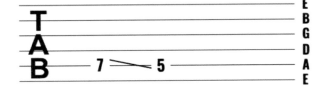

Vibrato

Vibrato involves creating a more or less subtle, oscillating pitch by "shaking" your finger up and down after pressing and playing a note on a specific fret. This technique mimics the effect of multiple tiny bends in quick succession. In tablature, vibrato is typically indicated by a slight wave symbol following the note.

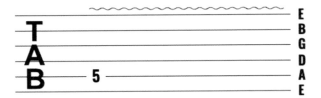

Chords

In guitar tablature, chords are notated by stacking numbers vertically on the six lines that represent the strings. Each number indicates which fret to press on the corresponding string. When the numbers are aligned vertically, it means the notes should be played simultaneously, forming a chord.

The clefs

In music notation, clefs are symbols used for reading and writing music. The bass and treble clefs are the most familiar ones, showing different pitch ranges on a staff. These clefs give musicians a clear picture of the notes' pitch, helping them read and perform music correctly.

Treble Clef
In piano sheet music, the treble clef represents notes above middle C, typically played with the right hand. It's often referred to as the "G" clef due to its resemblance to the letter "G."

Bass Clef
The bass clef denotes notes lower than middle C. It's also known as the "F" clef, resembling the letter "F," with its dots centered on the line for the note "F." In piano sheet music, the left hand usually plays notes in the bass clef.

Sight reading chart
Reading notes involves knowing the pitch based on their position on the musical staff. The treble clef represents higher notes above middle C, and the bass clef represents lower notes below middle C. See the visualized notes for each clef below.

SIGHT READING CHART

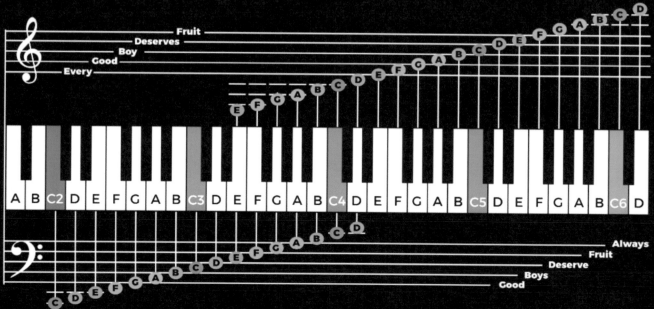

Notes and values

In music, notes and their corresponding rests are represented using unique symbols. Western music typically divides compositions into measures, often consisting of four beats.

While we'll explore time and rhythm more comprehensively in the next lesson, let's discuss note appearances and their values. Please refer to the visual table below for a clear depiction of notes and their durations, which are mathematically structured as follows:

- **Whole notes** last for 4 beats in common time (4/4).
- **Half notes** endure for 2 beats in 4/4 time, akin to two halves of a whole note.
- **Quarter notes** are held for 1 beat and can be subdivided from a half note.
- **Eighth notes** are held for half a beat and can be subdivided from a quarter note.
- **Sixteenth notes**, held for a quarter of a beat, can be subdivided from an eighth note.

Name	Note	Rest	Length
Whole note	𝅝	▬	4 beats
Half note	𝅗𝅥	▬	2 beats
Quarter note	♩	𝄽	1 beat
Eighth note	♪	𝄾	1/2 beat
Sixteenth note	𝅘𝅥𝅯	𝄿	1/4 beat

Connected notes

In music notation, you'll notice that some notes have tails and others are linked together. These tail shapes indicate the duration of the notes. When notes have a rhythmic value less than a quarter note, such as eighth and sixteenth notes, they can be connected, a practice known as 'beaming.' This beaming of notes is an essential element in notation that helps convey rhythm and duration, making it easier for musicians to read and play accurately.

Connected notes, like eighth or sixteenth notes, are visually grouped by joining their tails. This grouping simplifies the reading of complex rhythms, presenting a clear pattern instead of individual notes.

- **Eighth notes** are connected by a single line.
- **Sixteenth notes** are connected by two lines.
- **Thirty-second notes** are connected by three lines.

For a visual representation of these notes and their rhythmic values, please refer to the table below. This illustration provides a clear depiction of how these notes appear on sheet music, helping you understand their durations and relationships.

Name	Note	Beam	Length
Eight notes	♪♪♪♪		2 beats
Sixteenth notes			1 beat
Thirty-second notes			1/2 beat
Sixty-fourth notes			1/4 beat

Dotted notes

Dotted notes in music notation are regular notes with a dot to the right of their note head, extending their duration by half. For instance, a dotted quarter note equals three eighth notes, and a dotted half note equals three quarter notes.

For example, if you have a dotted quarter note, its duration is equivalent to a quarter note plus half of a quarter note, making it the same as three eighth notes. Similarly, a dotted half note is as long as a half note plus half of a half note, which equals three quarter notes.

Dotted notes in music have a dot to the right of the note head, extending their duration by half. In 4/4 time, a regular quarter note is one beat, but a dotted quarter note is one and a half beats. This adds complexity and character to music patterns. Here's a visual representation:

Name	Note	Rest	Length
Whole note			6 beats
Half note			3 beats
Quarter note			1½ beat
Eighth note			3/4 beat
Sixteenth note			3/8 beat

Key takeaways

Now that you have a grasp of basic music notation, you're on your way to becoming musically literate. As mentioned earlier, we've covered only the fundamentals of musical notation. With this knowledge, it's beneficial to seek out sheet music for your favorite songs. This will allow you to delve deeper into reading notes from both the bass and treble clefs.

Musical notation

Musical notation is a system of symbols used to write down and communicate music. It includes notes, clefs, and other symbols that represent pitch, rhythm, and various musical elements. Musicians read these symbols to perform and understand music accurately.

Treble clef

The treble clef, or "G clef," is for higher-pitched instruments and voices. It begins on the staff's second line (representing the note G) and is used for piano's right hand, violin, flute, soprano, and tenor voices.

Bass clef

The bass clef, or "F clef," starts on the fourth line (noting the F pitch) and suits lower-pitched instruments like piano's left hand, cello, tuba, and alto and bass voices.

Note values

In music, notes represent both the pitch and duration of a sound. The length of a note determines how long it is held or played, contributing to the rhythm and timing of a musical piece.

Jargon guide

Music theory can be a complex subject, and even more so with its specialized vocabulary. This guide is here to assist you in comprehending and defining the terms you've come across in this chapter or to refresh your memory.

Tablature

Tablature is a notation system primarily used for stringed instruments like guitar and bass. Instead of traditional music notation, it uses numbers or symbols to indicate where to place fingers on the instrument's frets or strings.

Hammer-ons

A technique where a finger is quickly pressed onto a fret to sound a note without plucking the string again.

Pull-offs

A technique where a finger is lifted off a fret to sound a lower note, without re-plucking the string.

Slides

A technique where a finger is slid along the string from one fret to another, producing a smooth transition between notes.

Bends

A technique where a string is pushed or pulled sideways on the fretboard to raise the pitch of the note.

Staff

A staff is a set of horizontal lines and spaces on which musical notation is written. It provides a visual representation of the pitch and timing of musical notes and symbols.

Measure

A measure (or bar) in music is a segment of time containing a specific number of beats. Measures help organize music into regular rhythmic patterns, with a barline marking the end of each measure.

Rest

A rest in music notation indicates a period of silence or a pause where no sound is played or sung. Rests are used to define the timing and rhythm of a composition.

Beaming

Beaming in music notation involves grouping together a series of adjacent notes with horizontal lines called beams. This helps visually clarify rhythms by showing which notes are played in a single beat or within a specific time duration.

Dotted notes

Dotted notes are musical notes with a dot placed to the right of the note-head. The dot extends the duration of the note by half of its original value. For example, a dotted half note is equal to a half note plus a quarter note.

Intermediate　　 **+/- 40 min**　　 **7 sections**

8. RHYTHM & TIME
THE PULSE OF MUSIC

Up next, we're delving into the intriguing world of rhythm and timing in music, where music takes on a mathematical dimension.

In this section, we'll explore how rhythm and timing serve as the vital pulse of music, shaping its expression and groove.

Join us as we unveil the mysteries of rhythmic patterns, time signatures, and syncopation, enabling you to connect with the heartbeat of music in a profound way.

‹ WHAT YOU WILL LEARN

- BPM
- The musical grid
- Musical meter
- Time signatures

‹ WHAT DO YOU NEED

- Any DAW
- A metronome
- MIDI Keyboard

‹ SKIP THIS CHAPTER IF

- You understand BPM
- You know what bars are
- You understand time signatures
- You understand musical meters

Guide to rhythm

Understanding rhythm is crucial in music. It might seem complex initially, but we'll simplify it for you. You'll learn how rhythms are divided, grasp time signatures, and explore compound and odd time signatures. Rhythm is music's organized heartbeat, grouping beats in a pattern at a tempo. Musicians use it for harmonious play.

Beats per minute

First, let's discuss BPM, short for 'beats per minute,' which determines the speed of your music. In music software, you'll hear clicks when you press play, with one louder click marking the starting point of each measure.

Bars

You might have come across rappers exclaiming "bars!" in their lyrics. A bar, in this context, refers to a musical phrase that comprises four beats. In the context of a 4/4 time signature, the most prevalent in music, each beat is always marked by a single metronome click.

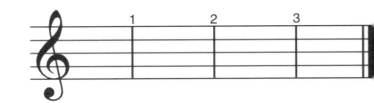

Time signatures

In music, the time signature indicates the number of beats in a bar. In 4/4 time, the most common signature, there are four beats. At 60 BPM, each click represents one beat in a 4/4 bar. So, after four clicks, you've completed one bar of music.

Time is your grid

To understand how time in music works, you have to see time as a grid. Within this grid (or time signature) is where our notes are placed. In a 4/4 time signature, you have the flexibility to position your notes on any beat or count, or even in spaces between the beats, allowing for a range of rhythmic possibilities. This grid-like structure offers a framework within which musicians can craft diverse rhythms and patterns.

In its simplest essence, music can be understood as a collection of notes strategically positioned on a grid-like framework. These notes can be combined to create chords, arranged sequentially in arpeggios, or even placed in a more unstructured manner to form melodies and rhythms. This fundamental arrangement of notes on a grid underpins the entire structure of musical compositions.

Grid inside a DAW

When observing a 4-bar musical phrase in the context of 4/4 time, the resulting visual resembles a grid. The highlighted yellow bar signifies the entirety of the 4-bar phrase. This yellow bar comprises four distinct sections, which correspond to individual bars. Below this visual representation lies the grid where musical notes find their placement.

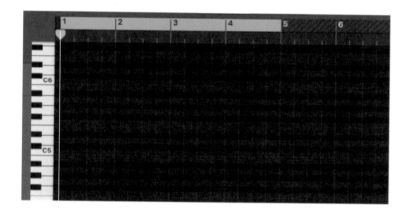

Grid on sheet music

When you examine a sheet of music arranged in a 4/4 time signature, you'll encounter a visual representation resembling a structured grid. You'll also notice vertical lines dividing the composition into distinct bars, while a double line serves as a conclusive marker, indicating the conclusion of the musical phrase.

Rhythm and notes

In music, rhythm is like the arrangement of notes on a grid, and beats are the steady heartbeat of the rhythm. It's good to know that these notes can mean different things depending on how long they last. A whole note is the longest, but it can be split into halves, quarters, eighths, and sixteenths. A half note lasts half as long as a whole note, and a quarter note lasts a quarter of the time a whole note does. It's kind of like dividing things up into smaller pieces while keeping the rhythm going.

Whole Note
A whole note is the longest in terms of duration, always lasting for the entire duration of a beat.

Half Note
A half note lasts for half the duration of a whole note. It's often counted as two beats in common time.

Quarter Note
A quarter note lasts for one-fourth the duration of a whole note. It's commonly used as the basic time unit and typically gets one beat in common time.

Eighth Note
An eighth note lasts for one-eighth the duration of a whole note. It receives half the duration of a quarter note, so it's often played twice as fast as a quarter note.

Sixteenth Note
A sixteenth note lasts for one-sixteenth the duration of a whole note. It's typically played four times as fast as a quarter note.

Musical heartbeat

Imagine as you stroll down the street, your footsteps become the heartbeat of your movement. Each time you take four steps, you complete a musical "bar" in this rhythmic journey. Now, the art of creating music becomes as simple as harmonizing your voice, rapping, or playing an instrument in sync with your footsteps, which serve as the underlying rhythmic pulse.

All music has a steady beat, like a heartbeat. This beat is measured in chunks of time called "bars" or "measures." In Western music, the time signature (4/4 symbol) of a song tells us how many beats are in each measure/bar, and the tempo tells us how fast the beat goes. This speed is what we call "beats per minute" or BPM.

When writing music on sheet music, the bars or measures represent the grouping of beats, and the time signature indicates how many beats are contained within each bar. This information is also visually represented in Digital Audio Workstations (DAWs) used for music production.

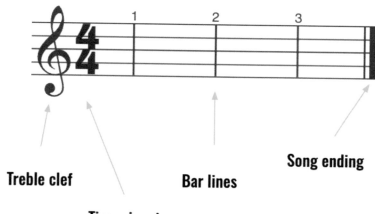

Treble clef

Time signature

Bar lines

Song ending

Exploring time signatures

Changing the time signature of a song significantly alters its rhythm and overall feel. In a 3/4 time signature, there are three beats in each bar, and each beat is counted as a quarter note. This gives the music a different rhythmic pattern compared to the more common 4/4 time signature, where there are four beats in each bar. The choice of time signature can greatly impact the pace, emphasis, and overall character of the music.

Strong and weak beats

In music, think of a bar like a mini rhythm cycle. It has both strong beats that push the rhythm ahead and weaker beats that balance it out. This mix of strong and weak beats helps us feel the rhythm better.

In a common 4/4 bar, the first and third beats are strong, like a little jump, while the second and fourth beats are softer. This blend makes the rhythm interesting and easy to follow.

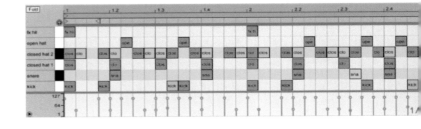

In music, it's like a rule that the thumping sound of the kick drum usually happens on the first and third beats. And the snare drum, which makes that sharp sound, often comes in on the second and fourth beats. This helps make the rhythm catchy and easy to feel.

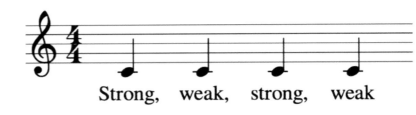

Strong,   weak,   strong,   weak

In a musical context where we're working with a 3/4 measure, the robust beat lands gracefully on the opening quarter note, while the subsequent two beats assume a gentler, more subdued character.

As you become accustomed to recognizing the distinctive tones of strong and weak beats within a musical measure, you'll notice their presence all around you. It could be the rhythmic thump of a kick drum in a 4/4 track, following a one-two, one-two pattern, or the rhythmic sway of a waltz with its gentle one-two-three, one-two-three flow.

Music meter

Think back to the footsteps analogy. Now, imagine if you took the time between steps and divided it into smaller steps of twos or threes, we call this idea 'meter'. It's like breaking down beats into smaller parts to create rhythms. The lower number of the fraction number is what we call the meter.

Meter in music refers to a regular pattern of strong and weak beats that forms the underlying rhythm. This rhythm is indicated at the beginning of a piece with a time signature. A time signature is written as two numbers, like a fraction. The top number shows how many beats are in each section of music, while the bottom number indicates the type of note that represents one beat. These note types include whole notes, half notes, quarter notes, eighth notes, and more, each representing different values.

Types of meters

Meter in music can be grouped into three categories: simple, compound, and complex. These labels help us understand rhythm in Western music. The key to these categories is how beats are divided. The number of beats in a measure determines which category of meter we use.

Type	Time signature	Beat unit	Beat division
Simple Duple	2/4		
Compound Duple	6/8		
Simple Triple	3/4		
Compound Triple	9/8		
Simple Quadruple	4/4		
Compound Quadruple	12/8		

Examples of 3/4 time signature

To grasp music meters, let's connect them to familiar songs. The following collection features songs in 3/4 time, known as waltz time. With three beats per measure, it mirrors the graceful waltz dance. Picture yourself waltzing to these rhythms.

By scanning the QR codes, you can listen to these songs and experience their livelier tempo. This liveliness sets them apart from the more common 4/4 time signature found in mainstream music.

The Weeknd - Earned It (3/4 time)

Alicia Keys- Fallin' (3/4 time)

Stephen Marley - Walking Away (3/4 time)

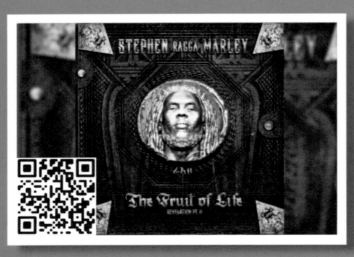

Metallica - Nothing Else Matters (3/4 time)

Examples of 4/4 time signature

Let's explore music rhythms using familiar songs. The songs listed below are in a 4/4 time signature, which is like a musical default. It has four beats in each measure, with the first beat being strong. This rhythm is the foundation of many songs we hear.

Imagine tapping your foot to the beat of these songs—it's like a steady heartbeat. If you scan the QR codes, you can listen to these songs and notice how they have a balanced and easy-to-follow rhythm. This rhythm is widely used in popular music, giving it a comfortable and familiar feel.

Black Eyed Peas - I Gotta Feeling (4/4 time)

Michael Jackson - Billie Jean (4/4 time)

Marvin Gaye - Let's Get It On (4/4 time)

Rihanna - Diamonds (4/4 time)

Examples of 2/4 time signature

The songs below use a 2/4 time signature, which is simple and clear. With two beats in each measure, the first beat is strong and the second is a bit lighter. This rhythm is often in lively music like marches.

Imagine dancing to these songs with quick steps. If you scan the QR codes, you can listen to these songs. They sound fast and energetic, creating a different feeling compared to the more common 4/4 time signature in popular music.

The Beech Boys- Surfin' USA (2/4 time)

Outkast- Hey Ya (2/4 time)

Bellinda Carlis - Heaven On Earth (2/4 time)

ACDC - Highway To Hell (2/4 time)

Key takeaways

In our exploration of Rhythm & Time in music theory, we've ventured into the heartbeat of music itself. We've uncovered the mathematical precision that underlies rhythm, realizing that it's not just an abstract concept but a crucial element that shapes musical expression and groove.

Throughout this chapter, we've dissected rhythmic patterns and delved into the significance of time signatures. By doing so, we've provided you with the tools to feel and understand the pulse of music in a profound way.

The musical grid

Time and rhythm serve as a grid or framework in music, providing a structured way to organize and place notes. The way we divide the time determines the rhythm with the BPM determining the tempo of the music.

3/4 time signature

3/4 time is often associated with a waltz, a dance style characterized by its graceful and flowing three-beat rhythm. When you listen to or play music in 3/4 time, you can feel a natural "one, two, three" pattern, and this time signature is commonly used in various musical genres, including classical, folk, and popular music.

4/4 time signature

4/4 time is incredibly versatile and can be found in a wide range of musical genres, including classical, pop, rock, jazz, and more. It provides a straightforward and steady rhythm that is easy to follow, making it a popular choice for many compositions

2/4 time signature

2/4 time is commonly used in music that has a quick and marching-like feel. It's often associated with styles like marches, polkas, and certain folk dances. The simple and regular rhythmic pattern of 2/4 time makes it easy for musicians to keep time and maintain a steady beat, which is essential in music with a brisk tempo.

Jargon guide

Music theory can be a complex subject, and even more so with its specialized vocabulary. This guide is here to assist you in comprehending and defining the terms you've come across in this chapter or to refresh your memory.

Compound time

Compound time is a time signature in music that divides each beat into smaller, equal subdivisions. It typically features groupings of three rather than two, creating a complex rhythmic feel. Examples of compound time signatures include 6/8 or 9/8.

Odd time

Odd time, also known as irregular meter, refers to time signatures that have an unusual number of beats in a measure. Unlike common time signatures like 4/4, odd time signatures often have an odd number of beats, such as 5/4 or 7/8, which can create a distinctive and challenging rhythmic feel.

Common time

Common time is represented by the symbol "C" and is equivalent to the time signature 4/4. It signifies that there are four beats in a measure, and the quarter note receives one beat. It is one of the most frequently used time signatures in music.

Beat/count

A beat, often referred to as a count, is a regular, recurrent pulse in music that provides a sense of timing and rhythm. Beats are organized into measures, and they establish the basic temporal framework of a piece of music.

Phrase

In music, a phrase is a musical segment or section with a distinct beginning and ending. Phrases often consist of several musical sentences or bars and contribute to the overall structure and expression of a composition.

Sync

"Sync" is short for "synchronization" in music and refers to the alignment of musical elements, such as instruments or vocal parts, to play or sing together in time. It ensures that different elements of a performance are coordinated rhythmically.

Treble clef

The treble clef, also known as the G clef, is a symbol in music notation that indicates the pitch range for higher-register instruments and voices. It is used to notate notes higher in pitch and is typically found on the upper staff of a musical score.

Strong/weak beats

In music meter, strong beats are the emphasized beats within a measure, often marked by downbeats. Weak beats are less emphasized and typically fall on the upbeats. The pattern of strong and weak beats contributes to the rhythmic feel and groove of a composition.

Meter

Meter in music refers to the recurring pattern of strong and weak beats that organizes the rhythmic structure of a piece. It is indicated by the time signature and helps establish the overall feel and pulse of the music. Common meters include 4/4, 3/4, and 6/8, among others.

Intermediate   +/- 40 min   7 sections

9. CIRCLE OF FIFTHS
THE ULTIMATE THEORY TOOL

In this final chapter, we explore the history and practicality of the Circle of Fifths, a valuable tool for composers, introduced by Ukrainian composer Nikolay Diletsy in Grammatika.

Diletsy's intention was to provide a valuable tool to aid songwriters and composers in their creative pursuits.

The circle of fifths boasts a multitude of practical features that can greatly enhance your music composition. In this chapter, we'll dissect these features, allowing you to seamlessly incorporate them into your own songwriting routine.

‹ WHAT YOU WILL LEARN

- Circle of fifths
- Circle of fourths
- Relative keys
- Neighboring keys

‹ WHAT DO YOU NEED

- Pencil and paper

‹ SKIP THIS CHAPTER IF

- You understand the circle of fifths and fourths and know how to use it

The circle of fifths

The circle of fifths is a popular topic in music theory, something that comes straight to mind when we think about how music works. In this lesson, we'll explain what the circle of fifths is, how it works, and how you can use and apply it in music.

Think of the circle of fifths as a musical map. It helps musicians build chord sequences and create harmonious music. The circle shows different key signatures and their main notes, organized in a specific order.

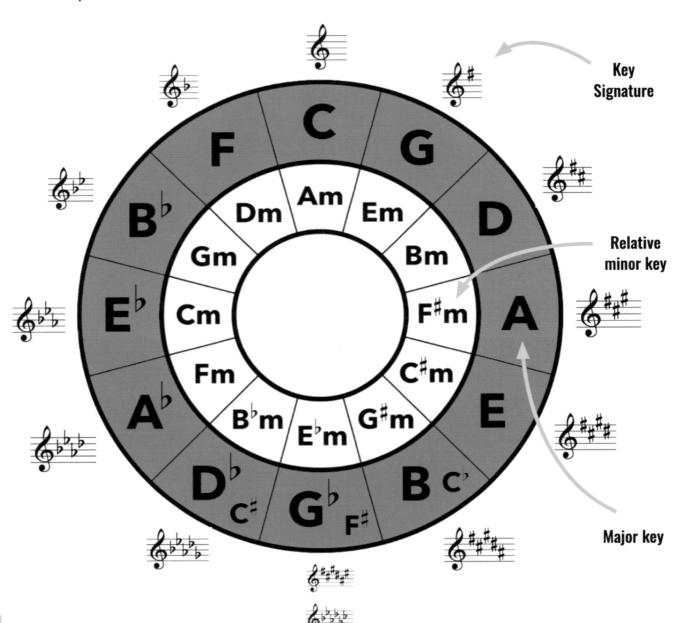

Key Signature

Relative minor key

Major key

About the circle

The most effective approach to help you grasp the workings of the Circle of Fifths is to guide you through the process of creating one yourself. So, let's get started with a simple exercise. Please take out a pencil and a sheet of paper to follow along.

Its as simple as drawing a clock. With the only difference being that the twelve marks correspond to one of the 12 major key signatures. At the position of 12 o'clock on our circle, We have C major, which serves as our fundamental key signature due to its absence of sharps or flats.

Let's shift our focus to the tick at one o'clock. How do we determine the key signature represented at this point? To help you visualize this, consider your piano or keyboard. Begin from the note C and ascend by seven half steps or semitones. You'll arrive at the note G. This interval of seven half steps is known as a perfect fifth.

Why does this matter? Well, every tick or key signature on the Circle of Fifths is precisely a perfect fifth apart from the preceding one. Consequently, the key signature located at one o'clock must correspond to G major. This is the reason behind the name "Circle of Fifths" – it's a visual representation of this recurring perfect fifth relationship. This is also why at one o'clock on some circle of fifths you'll notice one sharp circle.

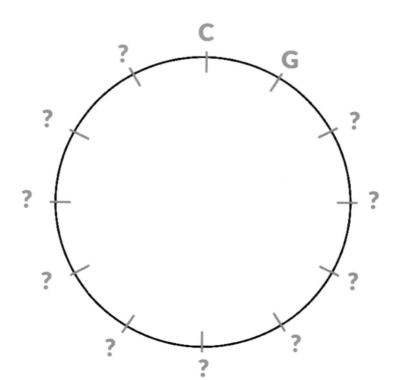

Around the clock

Once you realize that each tick of the clock represents a perfect fifth interval from the previous one, reading the clock becomes possible. Take a look at the circular illustration below to visualize how this concept translates to your piano keyboard.

Now, let's pinpoint the next key signature at two o'clock. If we leap up a perfect fifth from G, we arrive at D, indicating that our key signature at two o'clock is D major.

For our three o'clock key, continue the pattern by jumping a fifth above D, bringing you to A

Keep repeating this process, ascending by fifths, until you've assigned each of the 12 ticks with a Key signature. You've now identified all twelve major keys!

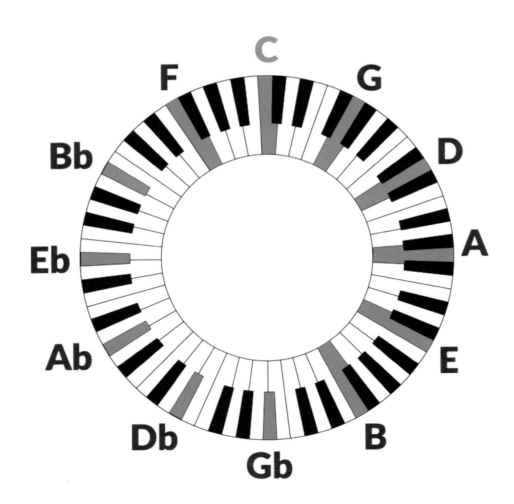

What the circle shows us

Each note on the upper part of the circle of fifths corresponds to a specific scale or key. For instance, at twelve o'clock, you have C, which represents the C major scale. Similarly, G represents the G major scale, and so on.

This arrangement on the circle signifies keys that are a perfect fifth apart from each other, offering immediate insights into which progressions are harmonically compatible.

For example, when you focus on the C in the circle of fifths, it allows you to craft a chord progression in the key of C major while providing a visual guide for identifying potential next chords in your composition.

For instance, if you were to form a triad chord for each note, you might begin at twelve o'clock with a C major triad. Then, you could move to the left to play an F major triad and proceed to G, where you'd play a G major triad.

This sequence consistently produces harmonious sounds because these keys are closely situated on the circle of fifths. In practical terms, transitioning from C to F to G forms a classic 1-4-5 chord progression, renowned as one of the most prevalent chord progressions in music.

On the circle of fifths, keys that are positioned closely to each other tend to yield more harmonious chord progressions. This is especially effective when selecting clusters of three keys, like C-F-G, for instance. Conversely, if you choose keys that are farther apart on the circle, your chord progression may sound less harmonious and connected.

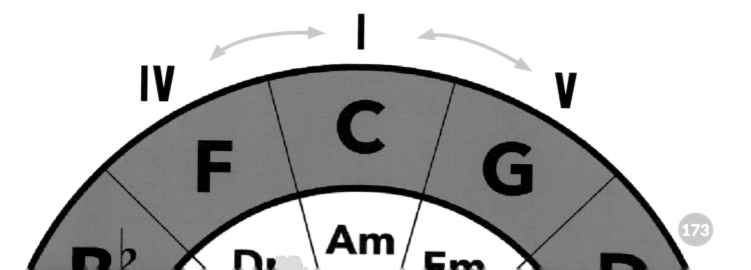

Keys with sharps

The circle of fifths offers a valuable advantage: it precisely indicates when we should incorporate a sharp or flat in each key. This is often shown on the outside of the circle.

To identify the keys requiring sharps, let's begin by moving clockwise around the Circle of Fifths, commencing at twelve o'clock, representing C major. As previously mentioned, C major doesn't include any sharps or flats.

The first sharp - G Major

To pinpoint the initial key that introduces a sharp, let's ascend by a fifth to G Major. When you play the Major Scale Pattern commencing from G, you'll observe that we need to include a black note—specifically, F sharp—to preserve the sequence of whole and half steps.

Moving further down - D Major

When applying this formula to the D major key, you'll discover that it entails two sharps—specifically, F sharp and C sharp. If you proceed in a clockwise direction around the Circle of Fifths, you'll observe that each successive key introduces an additional sharp until you reach the maximum count of seven sharps.

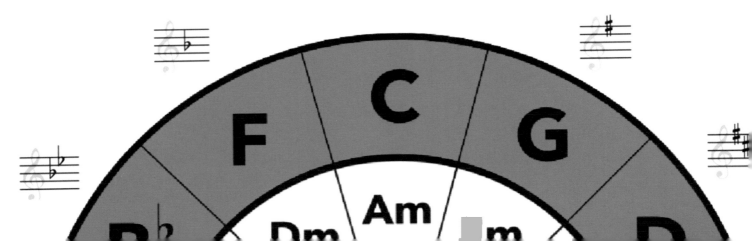

The circle of fourths

Now that we've explored all seven sharp key signatures, let's turn our attention to the keys featuring flats. How do we find those?

To locate the flat key signatures on the Circle of Fifths, we'll begin at C, which is situated at twelve o'clock, and move counterclockwise around the circle.

In terms of piano keyboard visualization, it's important to note that instead of ascending by a perfect fifth, as we do with sharp keys, when we move counter-clockwise, we descend by a perfect fifth or ascend by a perfect fourth

This is because G is the fifth note in C major, and C is the fourth note in G major. E is the fifth note in A major, and A is the fourth note in E major. When people talk of the circle of fourths, they are talking about the same thing, just counter-clockwise.

The first flat - F major
Now, let's play the Major Scale Pattern, beginning on F, and you'll quickly notice that to maintain the pattern, you'll need to include B flat. Now let's move further down to identify where the next flat is placed.

Moving further down - Bb major
To identify the subsequent flat key, simply descend a fifth or ascend a fourth from F, which brings you to B flat. When you replay the major scale pattern, you'll observe that you must incorporate a second flat on E flat to maintain the pattern.

Overlapping keys

Now that you're familiar with all the major key signatures, let's incorporate a keyboard into the circle of fifths and emphasize the notes utilized in C major. By highlighting both the notes in C major and G major, you can observe how the latter part of C major aligns with the initial segment of G major. This overlapping pattern repeats as you transition from G major to D major.

This really shows that all the scales in music are connected and form one big loop. Neighboring keys share connections with because they share some of the same notes. Composers like to use these shared notes to change the key of a piece to a nearby one. That's why you often see pieces using keys that are right next to each other on the circle of fifths. This connection of notes also applies to chords within each of these keys.

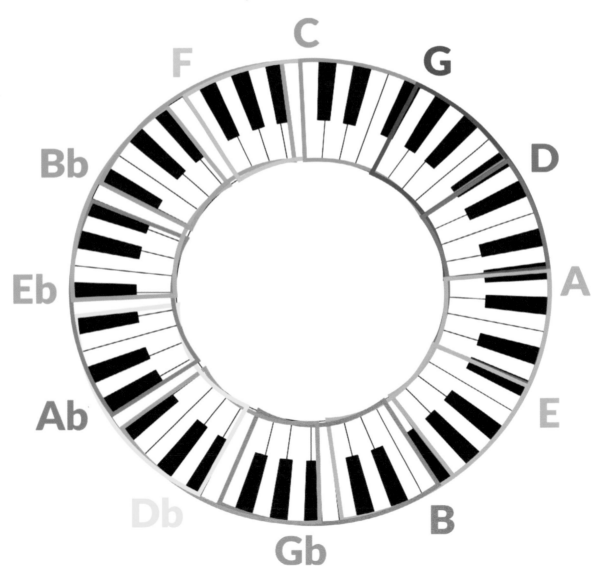

Minor keys

The circle of fifths not only introduces us to the major keys but also serves as a valuable tool for grasping the minor keys. It's a straightforward process since every major key has a counterpart known as the relative minor.

Let's revisit the lesson on scales where we discussed the concept of relative keys. As you've learned, you can identify the relative minor of a major key by either descending a minor third or ascending a perfect sixth.

You can determine the relative minor of any major key by moving down a minor third, equivalent to three half steps, from the starting note of the major key.

For example, starting from C and descending three half steps reveals that the relative minor of C major is A minor. Likewise, beginning on F will reveal that the relative minor of F major is D minor.

Similar to major keys, the order of minor keys also follows a progression by perfect fifths as you move clockwise around the circle of fifths.

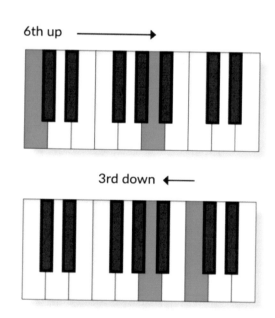

One of the remarkable features of the circle of fifths is its ability to provide instant insights into the relationships between major and relative minor keys. This eliminates the need for the often intricate process of identifying a major key's relative minor.

The circle neatly organizes this information for us, making it readily accessible. Right under each major key, you will find its relative minor key on the circle of fifths.

Relative keys

Let's discover the related minor keys for all major keys. For example, we learned that C major's relative minor is A minor because A is a minor third below C. In the same way, G major's relative minor is E minor. This pattern continues around the circle of fifths as we find relative minors for all major keys.

The great news is that each minor key shares the same number of sharps or flats as its corresponding major key. For instance, A minor and C major have no sharps or flats. Likewise, E flat minor and G flat major both feature six flats. This consistency simplifies understanding the relationship between major and minor keys.

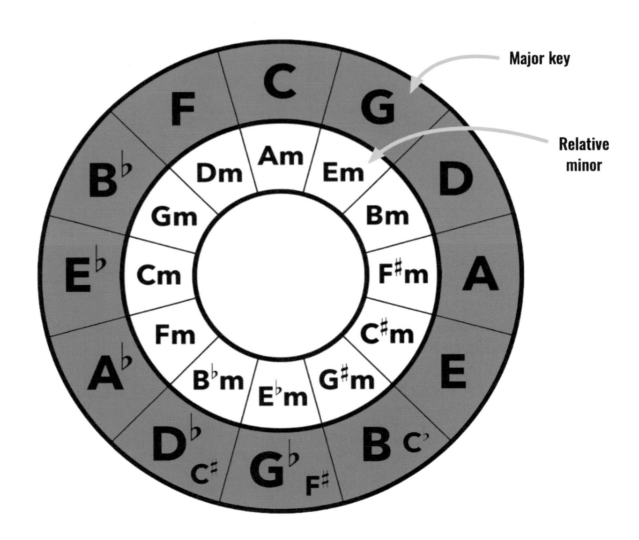

Major key

Relative minor

Key takeaways

In this chapter, we've dissected the elements of the circle of fifths, enabling you to apply its principles to your music composition. The circle of fifths serves as an invaluable reference tool for songwriting and beat-making.

It's crucial to keep in mind that while there are no strict rules in music, the circle of fifths provides valuable reference points. Feel free to explore your creativity extensively.

Key Relationships

The circle demonstrates the relationship between major and minor keys as well as the progression of key signatures in a sequence of perfect fifths (or perfect fourths if moving counterclockwise).

Sharps and Flats

As you move around the circle, you encounter key signatures with an increasing number of sharps or flats. This helps musicians understand which notes are naturally altered in each key.

Order of Sharps and Flats

The order of sharps and flats in key signatures is visually represented on the circle. The sequence of sharps and flats is crucial for understanding how key signatures are constructed.

Relative Keys

Opposite sides of the circle represent relative major and minor keys. This is important for understanding how major and relative minor keys share the same key signature.

Chord progressions

Leverage the circle of fifths to recognize chord progressions and hone your skills by experimenting with adjacent keys on the circle. It serves as a valuable guide for crafting harmonious transitions within your musical compositions.

Jargon guide

Music theory can be a complex subject, and even more so with its specialized vocabulary. This guide is here to assist you in comprehending and defining the terms you've come across in this chapter or to refresh your memory.

Nikolay Diletsky

Nikolay Diletsky was a Ukrainian composer and music theorist in the 17th century. He is known for his work in music theory, particularly his writings on the circle of fifths.

Key signature

In music notation, a key signature is a set of sharp or flat symbols placed at the beginning of a staff (the set of horizontal lines on which music is written). It indicates the key of a musical piece, specifying which notes should be played as sharps or flats throughout the composition.

Major key

A major key in music is a diatonic scale with a specific pattern of whole and half steps. It has a bright and happy sound and serves as a fundamental tonal center in Western music. Each major key has a relative minor key associated with it.

Minor key

A minor key in music is another diatonic scale with a different pattern of whole and half steps. It has a somber or sad sound, creating contrast with major keys. Each minor key also has a relative major key associated with it.

Key change

A key change, also known as a modulation, occurs when a piece of music transitions from one key to another. This change can be temporary or permanent and is used to add variety, emotional depth, or complexity to a composition.

Relative key

Relative keys are pairs of major and minor keys that share the same key signature. For example, C major and A minor are relative keys because they both have a key signature with no sharps or flats. Relative keys often have a close musical relationship, and composers use this relationship for creative purposes in their compositions.

Simplified circle of fifths

To enhance your understanding of the circle of fifths, we encourage you to explore our simplified version of the circle. This visual aid not only conveys the number of sharps or flats in each key signature but also highlights the specific notes requiring sharps or flats.

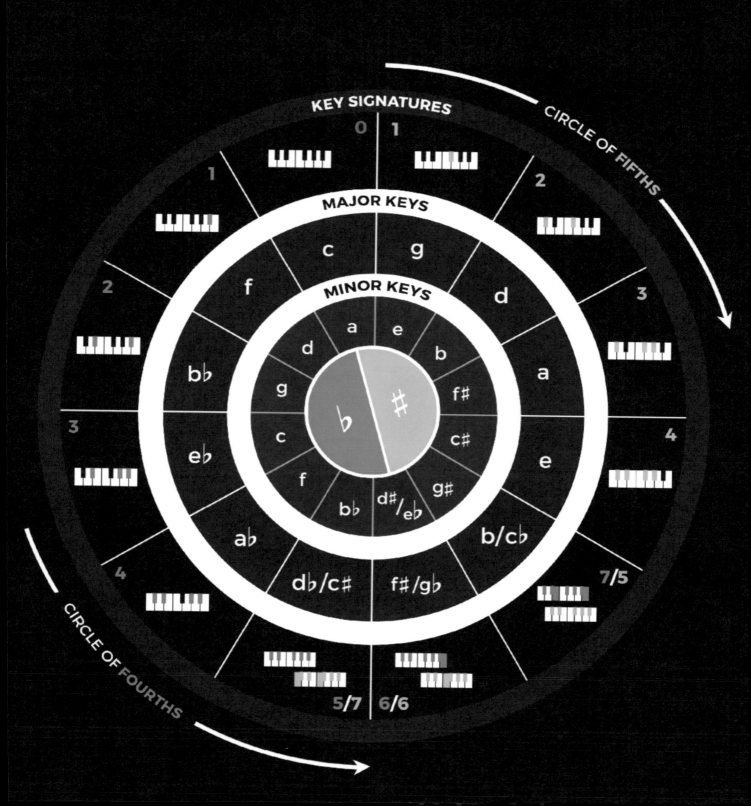

Author's note

Congratulations! You've successfully reached the conclusion of our book! As we wrap up Guitar Theory Simplified, I want to express my sincere gratitude for joining me on this musical journey. This book has been a labor of love, born out of the desire to make music theory accessible to all, regardless of background or experience.

I hope that your time spent reading this book has been as enjoyable and enlightening as my time spent creating it. Just as I've strived to inspire and guide through my music channel and Musiciangoods, I trust that you now have a stronger foundation to pursue your musical aspirations.

Feel free to reach out to me on social media if you have any questions about this book or music theory in general. I'm always open to your feedback, and I'm here to assist in any way I can. Your input is invaluable, and I look forward to being part of your continued musical exploration.

Our commitment to you includes regular content updates within this book, along with the addition of fresh lessons and video tutorials. By subscribing to our newsletter or following us on social media, you'll stay informed about the release of enhanced versions, available for free download. Your continued learning and growth in music are our priorities.

Don't forget to take advantage of the complimentary PDF cheat sheets provided with this book. You'll find them in the accompanying folder.

Thank you for being a part of this musical voyage, and I wish you all the best in your musical endeavors.

FOLLOW ME ON
Instagram: mrtellier

Complementary items

Enhance your music theory learning experience with the Guitar Theory Cheat Sheet Mouse pad, also available for bass guitar, from Musiciangoods at Musiciangoods.com. This unique mouse pad, along with the accompanying poster and digital PDF, visually presents key concepts from this book, making it a handy reference right at your fingertips.

If you're also interested in exploring music theory for keyboard instruments, we highly recommend our book Music Theory Simplified. Additionally, we also have a bass guitar edition of our book.

Simply scan the QR code to access these resources. As a valued reader, don't forget to use the discount code "theorysimplified" at checkout to enjoy an exclusive 20% off these essential tools.

XXL Back-lit version

Guitar chords chart

Guitar key chords guide

Music Theory Simplified

Made in the USA
Columbia, SC
23 June 2025

59750128R00104